828/WAT

The Passing of the Third-Floor Buck

KEITH WATERHOUSE

The Passing of the
Third-Floor Buck

London
Michael Joseph

First published in Great Britain by Michael Joseph Ltd
52 Bedford Square, London, WC1B 3EF
1974

ISBN 0 7181 1190 7

Set and Printed in Great Britain by
Northumberland Press Ltd, Gateshead
in Baskerville type eleven on twelve point,
and bound by James Burn at Esher, Surrey

Father, Mother and Me,
Sister and Auntie say
All the people like us are We,
And everyone else is They

RUDYARD KIPLING

The author wishes to thank the Editor and Proprietors of *Punch* for permission to reproduce material which originally appeared in its pages.

CONTENTS

1. The jungle book

Diary of a child guerilla

Monday, March 1, St. David's Day. Got up. Went to school. Came home. Had fish fingers. Went to bed. Started to count up to a billion but only got up to 7,643 for the reason that, my Father made me stop. He said that if he had to come up to my bedroom once more, that he would strangle me. This man is dangerous.

Tuesday, March 2, Got up. Had breakfast. Got ticked off by my Father for holding my Breath. People should not get ticked off for holding your breath, for the reason that, it is a free country. Therefore I hate my Father. He thinks he is somebody but he is nobody. Also he have hair coming out of the end of his nose.

Wednesday, March 3, Ember Day. I am going to get my Father. He has been asking for it and now he is going to get it. Just because I was sucking bread. He go purple and bangs the table. If he was Run Over I would be glad. He look like a Jelly and also is Smelly.

Thursday, March 4, moon's first quarter 3.01 a.m. Got up. Went school. Watched telly. Left roller skate on top of stairs, but, it did not work. This only works in comics such as Whizzer and Chips etc., therefore, comics are stupid. They, the people you are trying to get, do not step on the roller skate and go ker-bam-bam-bam-bam-bam-kkkklunk-splat-aaaargh. Instead of this, they just pick up the roller skate and say (This house getting more like a pig-sty every day.) He is Potty and also Grotty.

Friday, March 5, Today I said I was going to John's house but I did not, I went to the Pet Shop to buy a poisonous snake, but they did not have one. The copperhead, the Rattlesnake, the cobra and the Mamba are among the poisonous snakes to be found in the world. The man in the Pet Shop just laughed and tried to sell me a hamster. I am going to get him after I have got my Father.

Saturday, March 6, sun rises 7.35. I have got an Idea from watching Telly. It is where they were in a certain foreign country and he, the Tall one, invents this special kind of warfare. It comes to pass that this Warfare is something nobody else knows about, therefore he wins it. It is called (long word) warfare. (Long word) warfare is where, they do not fight with guns, tanks, also armoured cars, thus killing them, you fight a person's mind so therefore he will do what they tell them. It begins with the letter P. This I am going to do to my Father.

Sunday, March 7, 2nd in Lent, 1st day of Operation Stare. Operation Stare is where, you just look at your Father. You do not say anything, you just Look. This was when he was reading the paper, also when he was painting chest of drawers. He did not know I was there until, he saw me. I was just Staring at him. This is Operation Stare. It is (long word) warfare. It did not work, as he said (If you nothing to do you can tidy up your room). Another example of the poisonous snake is, the sea-snake. He has spots all on his neck. He is Spotty and also Potty.

Monday, March 8, On this important day I invented the art of making yourself cry. You have to pretend that you have a dog. This could be a Sheep-dog or numerous others, it is called Zebadee. You have to pretend that it runs away in the park and, you come to this swamp and it rescues you and die. After you have gone into the swamp to get it out, the (dog). It dies and you are sorry. This can make you cry, but my Father just say, (Stop snivelling or I will give you something snivel about).

Tuesday, March 9, Nothing happened. I am still going to get my Father. I will make him Crack.

Wednesday, March 10, birthday of Prince Edward. Today I got my Father to think that I could not move my left arm, also that I could not feel anything in it, it was Dead. I thought this would make him sorry and it did. He went all white and call me Son. He pinch my arm and asked if I could feel it, I replied that (I could not.) We had better see Dr. Murray!!! he exclaimed, but just as he was helping me on with my coat to go Dr. Murray, he sticks a pin in my arm accidentally on purpose. This hurt me so I said (Oh.) He went all purple and call me Lad.

Thursday, March 11, Got up. Decided to Lie Low.

Friday, March 12, full moon 3.34 a.m. On this day Operation Blink came into being. You just blink your eyes all the time, it drive him Potty. Also, at the same time, you must screw your nose sideways and also make your mouth go down, while you are blinking your eyes. I did this all the time, until my Father Went Out.

Saturday, March 13, An unlucky day for my Father. On this, the 2nd day of the famous victorious Operation Blink, he take me to see (The Railway Children). I was sick on the bus going, also in the cinema. When we came out, he asked, (Are you feeling better now). I replied that I was, therefore, we went on the bus. I was sick. My Father does not know it, but, I did it on purpose. I have discovered the art of being Sick. It is my secret. I was Sick all over his shoes. The (Railway Children) is a good picture, it better than Rolf Harris. He is Cracking.

Sunday, March 14, 3rd in Lent. Operation Blink and Operation Sick are still in being. I said I was going to Get him and I have got him. If you keep sniffling, he does not say anything but you can tell he does not like it, this big Vein stands out in his forehead and sort of goes throb-throb. This is Operation Sniffle. This morning I heard him say to Mr. Baker (Are they born like it or what, I don't know what I am going to do with him.) This means that I have won. He knew that I was holding my breath all through lunch time, but he does not say anything, he just Went Out. This also means, that I have won. Today I have started counting up to a billion and have got up to 10,500. I have got to get up to 25,000 before going to bed, or it will mean that I have lost the Battle. He has come back in and, he knows that I am counting up to a billion but, he is just staring at wall and drinking the whisky. It is 3.10 p.m. on Sunday, March 14, the day of Victory. He has Cracked, and must sign my Terms.

Play school

According to Hoyle, most popular children's games simply do not exist. I suppose this is because their participants, being naturally indolent or illiterate or preferring to climb trees instead of attending committee meetings, have never bothered to write down the rules. It is also true, I believe, that children tend not to congregate in the upper rooms of village pubs, where traditionally the laws of cricket, Association football, Rugby League, ice-hockey, poker and the remainder were drawn up on the backs of menus.

A pity, that, for how many games of conkers or hopscotch have been won by default through ignorance of the complex rules? How many children can recite the Declaration of Intent—a variation of the Hippocratic Oath—that was to have cleaned up the sport of doctors and nurses? What boy is aware of the first law of marbles, which is that although every tournament shall be played for keeps, no tournament shall really be played for keeps always provided that the loser shall throw himself to the ground, drumming his heels and screaming, 'Tisn't fair!'?

For want of a stub of pencil and half a page torn from an exercise book at the right moment, the rules of many children's games are lost in antiquity. This constitutional void has often led to unseemly behaviour on the field. A skipping marathon in East London, for example, recently broke up in disorder because none of the contestants could agree as to the order of the condiments in the skipping rhyme. An elimination standing-on-one-leg competition in Derbyshire was abandoned when one of the semi-finalists challenged the umpire's decision that holding onto the railings was not permitted. The Northern Long-distance Spitting League has been arguing for three generations as to whether the expectoration of licorice juice shall constitute a foul.

These are happily isolated examples. It would be a sad day if children's games in general began to acquire the same ugly reputation as soccer or chess. In order to avoid the escalation of unpleasantness in what should be healthy, competitive sports, I have attempted to jot down a few notes on some of the children's games I remember best. Perhaps some minuscule Hoyle will continue the good work and produce the definitive treatise.

Not Walking on the Cracks of Pavements

This is an essentially urban game, the object being to perambulate a measured stretch of pavement—usually to the nearest sweetshop and back—without stepping on the cracks. The origins of the sport are obscure but there is documentary evidence that it was played by Dr. Johnson, whose shambling gait was said to have been caused by over-meticulous play on a cobbled course.

Rules. 1. A crack in the pavement shall be interpreted as the gap between one paving-stone and another. Faults in the pavement surface or the edges of coal-hole covers are not cracks. 2. All players to set off simultaneously. 3. No bumping or boring. 4. It is permissible to negotiate the course on a scooter, but scooting over a crack will be declared a fault. 5. Last one to the sweetshop is a big sweaty nit.

A player shall be deemed to be dismissed when he or she steps on a crack. In the event of a player being so dismissed, the earth shall open up and swallow that player alive. The game shall continue until all but one of the players shall have been swallowed up alive.

Walking to the End of the Lane with Your Eyes Closed

This was originally a rural version of the game just described. It is said that many years ago a group of yokels were playing Not Walking On The Cracks in a certain village lane. One of them, more observant than the others, noticed that the country lane was not paved, hence that there were no cracks. To enliven what was necessarily a slow-moving match when played in pastoral surroundings, the yokels introduced a new rule: that all contestants must keep their eyes closed until they reach the end of the lane. Thus—in much the same way as Rugger evolved from Soccer when William Webb Ellis first handled the ball in 1823—an entirely new sport was born.

In essence, the rules of Walking With Your Eyes Closed remain the same as those for Walking On The Cracks, with appropriate adjustments for the variation just described. The most important of these is that a player being dismissed the game shall be carried off by a big furry monster and boiled in a pot, rather than being swallowed up alive as in the traditional version.

Counting up to a Zillion

There are many variations of this exacting sport, ranging from the simple Counting Up To A Million to the more sophisticated and energetic Counting Up To A Million Zillion Trillion. Counting Up To A Zillion has perhaps the most devotees.

Rules. 1. Each Player shall count in a high-pitched monotonous voice, beginning at nought (o) and not pausing for breath until he has reached one zillion (1,000,000,000,000,-000,000). 2. A player counting under his breath and then claiming to have reached twelve million shall be disqualified. 3. Counting in fives, tens or hundreds shall be disallowed. 4. The use of non-recognised or eccentric numbers such as fifty-twelve or eleventy-ten is not permitted.

A disadvantage of Counting Up To A Zillion is that like the Eton Wall Game it rarely ends with a definite result, the main reason being that it takes twelve years to complete a single innings.

Holding One's Breath

This is often played on Counting Up To A Zillion pitches when the presence of parents or elder sisters may have created unfavourable conditions for any game that cannot be conducted in absolute silence. The object of the game is to see which of a number of players can hold his breath longer than the others. The rules may be subject to many and diverse local variations, but there is a standard Non-Breathing Code laying down the circumstances in which one contestant may examine another to see if his heart has stopped beating. The Code also discourages babes-in-arms from taking part in this game, even as amateurs.

Is-Isn't-Is-Isn't-Is

Played with something of the ritual of Japanese wrestling, this is a battle of wits between two players, requiring great verbal dexterity.

The game commences with one of the players making a statement or *postulation*, e.g. 'The moon is flat' or 'My dad can beat your dad' or 'If you swallow chewing-gum it winds round your heart and you die'.

The challenger must then reply with the *response*, which according to the rigid customs of the game shall be 'It Isn't', or 'He can't' or 'You don't', according to which may be most appropriate.

The first player then counters with the *assertion*—'It is', 'He can', 'You do', etc. Immediately, the second player must produce the *contradiction*—'Isn't', 'Can't', 'Don't', etc. —else he shall have forfeited the game. Note that at this stage the *abbreviation* of the responses has been arrived at —'Isn't' instead of 'It isn't', and so on.

This style of play continues until one or other of the players shall introduce the *variation*. There are as many variations as there are moves in chess, and it is necessary to learn them by heart before one can hope to become an accomplished player. A simple sequence of variations might be as follows: —

'Is.'

'Isn't.'

'Is.'

'Isn't, you rotten stinker.' (First variation.)

'Rotten stinker yourself.' (Second variation.)

'Don't you call me a rotten stinker.' (Third variation.)

'Well you are one.' (Fourth variation.)

'Aren't.' (Fifth variation.)

'Are.' (New sequence commences.)

The game continues through many such sequences and concludes with the *assault*, when one player shall have been led to the point of hitting the other one in the mouth.

The debate goes on and on

On a motion, That in the opinion of this House, the novels of Evelyn Waugh are superior to the Monkees' recording of 'A Little Bit Me, A Little Bit You,' the House divided.

Opening the debate, the Father of the House expressed his concern at the amount of television that was being watched. Homework was not being done and an undertaking not to leave bits of plastic boomerang all over the dining-room table had not been honoured. The Members opposite seemed to spend their waking hours slouching about on the floor and listening to gramophone records. There was a need for change. At the age of the principal speaker for the opposition the Father of the House was reading *Scoop* by Evelyn Waugh instead of trashy comics, and was earning 3s. 6d. a week delivering newspapers. There was no television. Children perforce made their own amusements. If music was listened to it was good music and not rubbish.

Opposing the motion, the 11-year-old asked the speaker if he was familiar with the works of Monica Edwards. They were horse books. She could not understand authors— Evelyn Waugh had been mentioned—turning their talents to other subjects when horse books could be written. On the subject of newspapers, anyone who delivered them for 3s. 6d. a week was loopy. Newspapers themselves were loopy. People occupied hours reading newspapers that might be better spent riding horses. She would, however, give the House this undertaking: she would deliver newspapers for £10 a week if the Father of the House would repudiate a previous ruling that she could not have a bicycle. Emma Featherstone had a bicycle, as did Anne-Marie Wilcox. With a bicycle she could earn £10 a week delivering newspapers. The £10 would be invested in a horse. She would then deliver newspapers on horseback to anyone loopy enough to want them. Turning to music, she could only say that the music of the Monkees was good music and not rubbish. A poll had been taken at school and there had been unanimous agreement that the Monkees were fab. The only dissenting voice had been that of Anne-Marie Wilcox, who was wet. Anne-Marie Wilcox preferred the Beatles. The Beatles were wet.

Supporting the opposition speaker, the six-year-old recalled a period when she had been in favour of the Beakles. She had liked the Beakles but now she liked the Monkees better. The Monkees were better than the Beakles. The Beakles were not as good as the Monkees. She would ask the Father of the House if he did not agree that Batman was better than the Beakles.

The Father of the House replied that Batman was not at issue. He did not object to Batman within reason. What he did object to was trashy comics all over the house and a Coca-Cola bottle, the property of the last speaker, left on the stairs for anyone to trip over. He would put it to the Members opposite that they were not living in a pigsty.

Intervening, the three-year-old asked the Father of the House if he was Mr. Trousers. He personally was Mr. Wowsers. Amending this, he declared that he was not Mr. Wowsers, he was Mr. Blouses. No, he was Mr. Batman. No, he was Mr. Beakles.

The Father of the House said that he would like to put a serious proposition to the principal Member opposite. Would she just open *Scoop* by Evelyn Waugh and read the first page? At her age he had found it enjoyable. There was more in life than cutting out photographs of some scruffy group from *The New Musical Express*. There was also a need to fetch the Sellotape downstairs and put it where it belonged.

The 11-year-old said that the Monkees were not scruffy. The Rolling Stones were scruffy but this was for the reason that they were wet. Emma Featherstone's mother had a friend whose cleaning lady knew Cliff Richard's cleaning lady. By no stretch of the imagination could Cliff Richard be called scruffy. Emma Featherstone's bicycle, moreover, had a basket in front. Such a basket, which could later be adapted to a horse or pony, would be useful for carrying newspapers. On the question of Sellotape, she was confident that her colleagues could throw more light on the matter, as they had it last.

The six-year-old emphatically denied that she had seen the Sellotape. She had listened carefully to all that had been said, both for and against the Monkees. She would ask the Father of the House how golf-balls were made. She fully understood that there were factories where shoes, wood, meat and other articles were made and that these factories must also make golf-balls, but how did they make them round?

The Father of the House said he imagined that there were special machines. There would be a sort of round mould and various substances—rubber and so forth—would be put in this mould and it would reproduce a round golf-ball.

On a point of order, the three-year-old asked the Father of the House if he was Mr. Bolf-Ball. His colleagues were Mrs. Bolf-Ball and Mrs. Bolf-Beakles respectively.

Over-ruling the Member, the Father of the House said that they were straying far from the point. There was a need for stronger measures. The principal Member opposite had been asked in the nicest possible way to read one page of *Scoop*. She had chosen instead to read a trashy comic. He did not wish to lay down the law, but in future the Member's subscription to trashy comics would be cancelled. Bedtime would be strictly enforced. Records of scruffy pop-groups would not be played. Pocket-money would be cancelled.

Cries of 'Oh!'

The Father of the House then proposed the amended Motion: That the principal Member opposite should either start reading *Scoop* or go immediately to bed; that her colleagues should stop making that dreadful racket; and that whoever put a half-eaten apple on the bookshelf should remove it forthwith.

The Motion was defeated by three votes to one but on a recount—the Father of the House exercising three casting votes—was adopted.

A further amendment, That this House is Mr. Splodge, was defeated.

What shall we tell the parents?

Xmas Day minus 12, countdown begins. My Father keep asking me what I want Xmas. You cannot just have Parcels in this house, you have to make out a List. It go up the chimney, after he have crossed out Bicycle and also copied it out, he thinks I don't know but I do know, I have seen him. The list is supposed to go to Santa Claus. There is No Such Person.

Xmas Day minus 11. I have made out my List. I want a troch, bicycle, fort, Whizzer & Chips Annual, pen that lights up, That Game, as well as Box of Smarties, American jail-wagon, also Parcels. I would rather just have Parcels. In this house, the Things that you get, for Christmas, they are just put on the bottom of the bed so that, you can see them all at once, when you wake up. A person should not be able to see them all at once. They should be Parcels.

Xmas Day minus 10. (What on Earth is a blessed Troch?) vouchsafed my Father, at the same time reading my List.

(It is like a pen that, it lights up, but, it does not write) I ejaculated.

(Oh, a 'Torch') groaned my Father. (I have a good mind to ask Santa Claus to bring you a Blessed Dictionary).

(And another thing, what on Earth That Game when it is at home?) continued that worthy. (Is it Monopoly, Ludo, Snakes & Ladder, or what?)

(It is called, Mousetrap) I vouchsafed.

You should not begin a sentence with the word, And.

24

Also, you should not vouchsafe that, Santa Claus no room on his Sleigh for a bicycle, when, what you mean is, certain persons are too mean to buy one.

Xmas Day minus 9. Today my Father caught me looking in Linen Cupboard. (What you doing in there, lad?) he ejaculated, but, he did not say anything. This mean that, he has not bought my Presents, yet.

Xmas Day minus 8. Today my Father caught me looking in Spare Room. (If you do not stop prying and poking in, places that do not concern you) stormed The Latter, (I shall tell Santa Claus not to bring you any Presents). This mean that, he is going to Get them tomorrow.

If he could really talk to Santa Claus, you would not have to put List up chimney. Why should you have to post List up chimney, if you can talk to him. Elementary my dear Watson. There is No Such Person. It is Your Father.

Xmas Day minus 7. (By the way, lad) exclaimed my Father, (I do not think that Santa Claus can find you a Mousetrap Game).

This means that, he has Got Them.

Pouring himself a Whisky, my Father continued his narrative. (And Santa Claus wants to know, what Earth is a blessed American jail-wagon?)

(It is where the Sheriff puts them in, when they have been caught. The bullion robbers) I maintained, adding for good measure, (You can get them at Hamley's.)

(I am not going to blessed Hamley's again!) he vouchsafed quickly. He given himself away. It is Him all the time.

Xmas Day minus 6. My Xmas presents are in My Father's Wardrobe. I have found them. I have got, 1 troch, 1 fort, Box Smarties, 12 Soldiers, 1 pen that does not light up, Rotten Dominoes, also Pencil Box, also 1 Rotten Book. I have not got, 1 bicycle, 1 pen that lights up, 1 Whizzer & Chips Annual, 1 Mousetrap Game, 1 American jail-wagon. The Rotten Book is entitled, (The Children Encyclopedia). This is not a real Present, it is like School. Another example is, the Pencil Box. They should not say they are Presents, they should just give you them. In this house they do not just give you them, they crack on they are Presents.

There are no Parcels, they are just in paper bags from (Hamleys). This proves that there is No Such Place as Santa Claus's Workshop, Reindeerland, North Pole, The World, The Universe, Space, Outer Space, The Galaxy.

Xmas Day minus 5. Today My Father go Purple. (What been doing in my Wardrobe?) volunteered he, adding for good measure, (You prying little Monkey).

(I have not been in Your Wardrobe) vouchsafed I, but all in vain. (Then why there a Chair in front of it?) ejaculated my Host, adding for good measure, (You not deserve Christmas Presents, I am going to give them all away to the Poor Children).

He knows I have seen them, therefore, he will have to get me Some More, or, it will not be a surprise.

Xmas Day minus 4. He has taken them out of the Wardrobe. Also, they are not in linen cupboard, boot-hole or pantry. The tool-shed is another example. I will find them.

Xmas Day minus 3. Today, I asked my Father how Santa Claus, can take all the Presents round, when there are so many children, in the world. (Ah!) gasped My Father. (Most of the Presents are delivered by the Fairy Postman, and then Santa Claus drops the Rest of Them down the chimney on Xmas Eve).

This means, that, he has got Some More. He has got an American jail-wagon.

Xmas Day minus 2. They are in the Cistern Cupboard. I have not looked at them, as it would not be a surprise. I have just felt them, with my eyes closed. I think I have Broken the American jail-wagon.

Xmas Eve, blast-off. Tonight, I could not sleep. My Father kept looking round The Door. He looked round The Door at ten o'clock, half-past ten, eleven o'clock, twenty-past eleven, 10 to twelve, five past twelve, 25 past twelve, also one o'clock. He go all Purple and start shouting, (if you not asleep in ten minutes, I am going to ask Santa Claus not to come). I heard him opening Cistern

Cupboard door where he has Got Them. Also, I heard him vouchsafe to my Mother, (Next year he gets a sleeping tablet before he goes to bed). He is going to Drug me.

Besides the Other Things, I have got, 1 Mousetrap Game, 1 Whizzer & Chips Annual, 1 Set of Matchbox cars (got them already, if He did but know it), also 1 Detective Set. I will use this for Finding Things Out.

Xmas Day. Today I woke my Father at Five O'Clock by the means of shining my new troch in his eyes. (Look what Santa Claus has brought me) I volunteered. He Swore. This means, that he will go to Hell.

Later, he came down for Breakfast. He would not mend my American jail-wagon, or play Mousetrap. He is the same as Scrooge. (You go to all this trouble, and he not play with Things for five minutes) ejaculated My Father, adding for good measure, (We will know better next year). He say this, every year.

Why I like Christmas is, you can watch telly at, break-fast-time. You can watch (Tom and Jerry), also, (Santa Claus) but, it is not him, it is just somebody Dressed Up.

A family on my back

So it's come to this, has it: mass rallies in Trafalgar Square in the cause of family life. I can remember a more discreet era when such matters were only mumbled about in the privacy of billiard room or gentlemen's urinal. Family life, where it did exist, went on behind closed doors.

Nowadays, of course, it is impossible to switch on radio or TV without hearing a discussion on the subject, usually blatantly one-sided. Advice columns on what to do in the event of a bad trip are openly printed in family newspapers which addicts can buy from W. H. Smith and other fixers. Many pop songs, with their sly juxtaposition of key-words such as 'love' and 'baby', are deliberately encouraging the young to take up family life.

It would be surprising if there were any arrests at the Trafalgar Square demonstration, except possibly for flagrant wife-kissing or pram-pushing. But this is not, as we have by now almost been wooed into believing, because the police, and indeed the whole administrative apparatus behind them, are hooked on family life themselves. That is a fiction spread by self-confessed family men who for years have been infiltrating the media with their insidious propaganda.

Whatever you may have read or heard, there is nothing particularly new or fashionable about family life. The Victorians, with their curious double standards, were familiar with the habit. Indeed, behind the net curtains of their villas in the railway suburbs, they were at it all the time. Little was known of the harmful effects of family living in those days, and the cheap magazines quite innocently printed stories in which it was a subject for amusement or even sentimentality. It was the *Strand* magazine which first came alive to the dangers of this sickly cult. It tried to offset the effects with a series of wholesome yarns about a bachelor detective who indulged only in cocaine.

By the nineteen twenties, family life had declined almost out of existence. Cocktails, cabaret, jazz, and luxury liners that sank without trace were what the bright young things were looking for. In present-day parlance, it would have been regarded as 'square' to admit a hankering for a little bungalow, a three-piece uncut moquette suite, a bit of garden, a holiday in Frinton, and all the other paraphernalia by which the family man may be recognised.

Then came war. It was a time of shortages, spivs, blackouts, and Richard Attenborough screaming that he was too young to die. Who could blame a Biggin Hill navigator or Johnny-head-in-air for seeking to relieve the tensions of the battle in the only way available? Family life had swept America during the Prohibition. Now battalions of G.I. Joes were spreading it through the English countryside. There was a thriving black market in wedding rings, prams, photograph frames, pruning forks. Very soon utility wardrobes could be bought openly. The 'dear octopus' as family life had come to be known—for it was always an expensive habit—had begun to flex its tentacles.

Today, there are whole areas of London where family life is regarded as normal and even socially acceptable. In Hampstead, Finchley, Potters Bar, Holland Park and certain parts of Golders Green it is quite usual for addicts to organise play-groups, PTA meetings and 'dinner parties' without any thought that they are giving offence to decent people. Gardening equipment and recipes for boeuf Stroganoff are freely passed from hand to hand.

In the provinces, Birmingham, Liverpool, Bristol, Manchester and Basildon New Town are among the black spots.

In many of these areas, coded advertisements for the houses in which family life takes place appear in the newspapers. 'Fhold semi, mgge availb,' for example, means that a pusher is offering a house for sale, but only on the understanding that the addict remains hooked *for life*, and that he will have to continue paying for his fix for a period of up to 25 years.

Most of the telltale signs of addiction to family life are perhaps too well known to describe here. The plastic gnome in the garden, the bag of sweeties for young Adam or Emma stuffed shamefacedly into a briefcase, the nervous blinking of the eyes when overdrafts or interest rates are mentioned—all these are indications of a family man who is beyond help. It is well known too that there are certain words and phrases, such as 'Dunroamin,' 'O-level,' 'Anniversary,' 'Au pair girl' and 'I don't suppose you know a reliable student who wants to do a bit of baby-sitting,' which have a special meaning in what is known, to the initiated, as the family circle.

What there is less public information about is how to detect the symptoms of a craving for family life in young people who are not yet irrevocably hooked. Among girls, the most common sign is a symbolic ring, usually set with a small diamond, worn on the third finger of the left hand. This tells the pushers and fixers that she is in the market for G-plan furniture, candlewick bedspreads, literature concerning refrigeration and advice on contraception. Among boys, the early symptoms are harder to detect. Normally, a young man standing on a pub table, blind raving drunk and singing 'I'm getting married in the morning, ding dong the bells are gonna chime,' should be regarded as a potential addict.

One uses the term 'addict'; but is there any medical or statistical proof that family life is, in fact, addictive? Unfortunately the evidence is overwhelming. A survey carried out by the Registrar-General showed that among young couples who have begun to indulge in family life in their early twenties and thirties, imagining no doubt that they could give it up whenever they felt like it, the great majority remained hooked—or 'faithful,' to use family argot—until death did them part. There are isolated examples of strong-willed men and women who have kicked the habit, but the withdrawal process is grisly and expensive. The cure is never complete, and there have been frequent cases of patients relapsing into family life for a second, third or even a fourth time.

Whether family life is physically harmful is still in dispute. The incidence of men who go down with a coronary upon learning that their teenage daughters are in the pudding club is indisputably higher among family men than among those who have never indulged; so is indigestion, backache, alcoholism, and going purple in the face when the bath is full of tights and knickers. But the main argument against the habit is the immense cost, which can be frightening. The secret tongs, or building societies as they are known in this country, have grown incredibly rich on family addiction. It is not unknown for men to pay up to half their salaries to these societies, and the other half to the supermarket Mafiosa which, in the bland pretence of serving a consumer need, has built up an enormous organisation entirely for the purpose of selling breakfast cereals and other junk to the pathetic victims of the family cult.

When the demonstrators demonstrate and the pop-singers preach the 'values' of family life, it is well worth asking ourselves who is pulling the strings. Is it not significant that family life is rife in Peking and Moscow, and is it not doubly significant that self-confessed family men in America are now speaking of trade with Red China? Do not be surprised if the two powers are shortly trading baby powder for bamboo napkin rings.

Thicker than water

For this composition, you have to write about Your Family if you are in Group A, and A Day At The Zoo if you are in Group B. Even though I am in Group B, I can not write about A Day At The Zoo as, my Father will not take me. He said (Never again) when I asked him. This mean, that, even though I am not in Group A, my composition is about Your Family. My Father say, that it will not make any Blessed Difference, as it is like a Zoo in this House anyway. That my explanation.

Your Family is made up of, Yourself, Your Father, Your Mother, your brother and Sisters if, you have any. Your Grandma, Your Uncles, and also Your Aunties. Also, there is also Your Cousins, if you have any. I do not have any.

Your Father is the Leader of Your Family. He like a King in, the olden days. Sometimes he is cruel and stern, at other times, he plays with me, this is not often. His cruel tongue is feared throughout the dominion. An example of this is, if your nails have Plasticine in them, he say (Look at your fingernails lad, I could grow a vegetable marrow in them). If you do not clean them, he Show no Mercy sad to relate.

Your Mother looks After you. She does not do any Work, she just stays at home whilst, Your Father goes to Work. The reason for this is, so that she can look After you. This is done by washing your shirts, cooking, Buying cakes and biscuits, picking things up such as your Lorries, and many other reasons. If you do anything wrong she always say (Wait till Your Father get home), but, she does not tell him. She just say (Ive had a hell of a day), then My Father say (What kind of a day you think Ive had). Sometimes, Your Mother and My Father shout at each other. This is because, My Mother has had It right up to here, and, also, Your Mother gets right Up my Father's Wick. This is only sometimes, at other times it is not, happy to relate.

As I am an orphan I do not have any Brothers or Sister, but, if you have, they can be younger than you or older than you, or, they can be your Twins, so if, you have spilled some red stuff on Your Mother's dressing table, you can say it was not you, it was them. You cannot do this if you are not Twins, they know it was you.

If they are Older than you, you have to wear their Clothes when they, that is, their Clothes, are too small for them. Your Brother or Sisters. But, if they are Younger than you, they can do what like and, you get the blame for it. Simon Mathieson in Group A is an example of this. Therefore, I am glad that I do not have any Brothers or Sister. Also, my Father is also glad. He say (Never again).

Your Grandma can be Your Father's Mother or Your Mother's Mother, or, she can be both. This means that you have Two. I only have One. Your Grandma was married to Your Grandfather but, he is dead. He has some medals for bravery.

My Grandma has a moustache. If you say (Grandma, why you growing a moustache), she does not give you any Money, but, if you say (Grandma, why is your hair all nice and silver) she give you 10p. She always give me 10p.

After Your Grandma, there are Your Uncles. Your Uncles are My Father's Brothers, they can be fat or thin. I have 1 fat and 2 thin ones, as well as, my Uncle Adam. Everyone thinks that, Your Uncle has got to be older than you by law, but, this is not true, as, my Uncle Adam is younger than me. He is my Mother's Brother. Therefore, he does not give me any Money. Also, he is a

Thief. I gave him some Chewing Gum, but, only to lend, but, he kept it. This makes him a Thief.

My Uncle Terence give me the Most Money. He gave me 50p on My Birthday, 50p at Xmas, 10p also on Sep 17, that is, the same day. I can remember this because, it is in my diary. It is in code. The code for my Uncle Terence is Tafy, this is Fatty backwards, but, he does not know I call him that. If he did know, he would not care, for the reason that, he is always Laughing. He Laugh every time he come, as well as Singing. He always Wake me up. On Sep 17 he was singing (Good King Wencelas) at the front door, and when I opened it, he gave me 10p and say (Happy Xmas Young Man). Later on, he also gave me a drink of some Fawn Stuff and then he gave me 50p, stating (Here 10p for you). My Mother said (He has had one too many), so, she must have known he had already given me 10p. But, she did not tell him.

When my Uncle Terence goes Home, My Mother always say (Never again). This my Father's saying. She has copied it. This mean that she is a Copy-cat.

After my Uncle Terence, there is lastly, my Uncle Edwin, and 2ndly, my Uncle Roger. They are both thin. My Uncle Edwin used to give me 5p, but he not come anymore, sad to relate. The reason for this is, My Mother said (I will not have him in house) and also, (If he come, I go) to My Father. I think My Uncle Edwin has a Disease, as My Mother say (He ought to see a Dr.) Last time he came, My Father was not in. We had cherry pie, this is my favourite. When My Father came home, my Uncle Edwin had gone home. My Mother said (What wrong with him, he cannot keep his clammy hands to himself.) Therefore, I bet he took 2 pieces of cherry Pie instead of 1 piece.

My Uncle Roger live in Australia, invented by Captain Cook. Much wool is to be had. He does not come to our house, he not send me any Money sad to relate, just a Koala Bear when I was 4. I cut it open, but there was no Money. When Your Uncle is in Australia, it is the same as being Dead.

Some people have Uncles, but, they are not really their Uncles. Simon Mathieson in Group A is another example of this. His Father is in Africa where, much Gold is to be got, but, his Uncle Arthur has come to stay with them. I know this because he has told me this. He is not really his Uncle, his Mother met him in a Pub, she say (This your Uncle Arthur). His Uncle Arthur is always giving him Money, I wish that I had one.

After Your Uncles, there are Your Aunties. Your Aunties are married to Your Uncles, but, these do not have to be Your Father's Brothers. They can be anybody, so long as, Your Aunties are Your Mother's Sisters. But, they are still your Uncles. The people they are married to.

I have 3 Aunties, 1 of them is married to my Uncle Terence, 2 of them are not. They can be old or young, these individuals are both.

My Auntie Nellie is the one whom, she is married to my Uncle Terence. She sometimes come looking for him, when, he is Out. She say (Has Terence been round, I not seen him for 2 days). My Mother say (No). She say (It getting too much of a Good Thing). My Auntie Nellie does not give me any Money, but, this is because she has not got any, as, my Uncle Terence does not give her any Money. This is what she told My Mother. It is because, he gives it to me happy to relate.

My other 2 Aunties are both Girls. They are both at College. They always come with different Men, but, these are not My Uncles. They have long hair, the different Men. My Father always call them Mick Jagger, when they have gone he always say, (He could do with a good Wash). They never give me anything, but, one of the different Men play with my Jigsaw also my Lego bricks, he said that they were Fantastic. He made a Lego Necklace for my Auntie Caroline, but, I would not let her keep it. She call me a Little Horror.

Once my Auntie Caroline came to stay with a different Man, not the same one, but a different one. He was supposed to sleep in my bed, and, I was supposed to sleep in the truckle-bed, but, he did not. He Got Up and, upon seeing that I was Awake, he stated (I am just going for a Leak) but, he did not come back. He went to finish the Jigsaw with my Auntie Caroline, they were Doing It all night. In the morning, My Father said (Never Again).

That is all that I have found out about Your Family, so far.

2. *Many inventions*

Electricity I have known

You learn something new every day. With no thought of
self-improvement, for example, I was reading that story of
Thurber's in which he recalls his mother's belief that
electricity leaks out of any empty light socket if the switch
has been left on. From this I gathered—going by the
general context, and the known fact that Thurber was a
humorist—that it doesn't.

I picked up another piece of electrical knowledge in
1951, while working as a drama critic on the *Yorkshire
Evening Post*. Wanting to imply that a certain actress had
given a muted performance, I wrote that while undoubtedly she had an electric presence, on this occasion it was
as if the electricity had been immersed in water. A kindly
sub-editor explained to me that when electricity gets wet,
by some miracle of the elements it intensifies rather than
diminishes. I have never seen the sense of this, but I con-
ceded the point and have used only gas-driven metaphor
since that date.

I was never taught electricity at school, nor was it often
a topic of dinner-table conversation among my parents.
What I know about the subject I have mastered the hard
way. Take, as an instance, television, an electrical device
of awesome complexity. Unlike more privileged students,
who are able to go running to m'tutor every time the frame-
hold goes wobbly, I have had to learn in the School of Life
that on the large rented model the knobs are on the front

whereas on the HMV portable they are on the side. Similarly with electric irons. When I bought my first electric iron there was no plug attached, presumably in case I wanted to wind the flex around my neck and jump off Westminster Bridge with it. There was a leaflet explaining how to get the plug on, but this was of course in German, the international language of the household appliances industry. Only by putting my natural intelligence to the problem did I eventually work out the solution—find a German-speaking electrician.

And so, what with having perforce to change a light bulb here and tune in a transistor radio there, I have picked up a pretty sound working knowledge of electrical matters. It is not comprehensive, God knows—I still can't fully understand why you can't boil an egg on an electric guitar—but when I jot down a summary of what I have learned, I marvel that I have never been asked to write for the *Electrical Journal*:

1. Most electricity is manufactured in power stations where it is fed into wires which are then wound around large drums.

2. Some electricity, however, does not need to go along wires. That used in portable radios, for example, and that used in lightning. This kind of electricity is not generated but is just lying about in the air, loose.

3. Electricity becomes intensified when wet. Electric kettles are immune to this.

4. Electricity has to be earthed. That is to say, it has to be connected with the ground before it can function, except in the case of aeroplanes, which have separate arrangements.

5. Electricity makes a low humming noise. This noise may be pitched at different levels for use in doorbells, telephones, electric organs, etc.

6. Although electricity does not leak out of an empty light socket, that light socket is nevertheless live if you happen to shove your finger in it when the switch is at the 'on' position. So if it is not leaking, what else is it doing?

7. Electricity is made up of two ingredients, negative and positive. One ingredient travels along a wire covered with red plastic, and the other along a wire covered with black plastic. When these two wires meet together in what we call a plug, the different ingredients are mixed together to form electricity. Washing machines need stronger electricity, and for this a booster ingredient is required. This travels along a wire covered with green plastic.

8. Stronger electricity cannot be used for electric razors. Electric razors make a fizzing sound when attached to a power plug.

9. Electricity may be stored in batteries. Big batteries do not necessarily hold more electricity than small batteries. In big batteries the electricity is just shovelled in, while in small batteries (transistors) it is packed flat.

10. Electricity is composed of small particles called electrons, an electron weighing only $1/1.837$ as much as an atom of the lightest chemical element, hydrogen, unless the *Encyclopaedia Britannica* is a liar.

Incurious people are content to take all this as read. They press a switch and the light comes on, and that is all they know about the miracle in their homes. This has never done for me. I have to know how things work, and if I cannot find out from some technical handbook—the *Every Boys' Wonder Book* series does an advanced manual on electricity—then I combine such information as I already have with simple logic. Thus it is very easy to deduce that the light switch controls a small clamp or vice which grips the wires very hard, so that the electricity cannot get through. When the switch is flicked on the vice is relaxed and the electricity travels to the light bulb where a bit of wire called the element, is left bare. Here, for the first time, we can actually *see* the electricity, in the form of a small spark. This spark is enlarged many hundreds of times by the curved bulb which is made of magnifying glass.

Why, is our next question, do these light bulbs have a limited life? As any schoolboy knows, heat converts oxygen into moisture. When all the oxygen in the light bulb has become liquified in this manner, it naturally quenches the electric spark. Some years ago a man in Birmingham invented an everlasting electric light bulb which, since it contained no oxygen, would never go out. The rights in it were bought up by light-bulb manufacturers who keep it locked in their safe.

Now we come to electricity as a source of power rather than a source of light or heat. Why, when you plug in an electric iron, does it get hot, whereas when you plug in an electric fan it does not get hot but whirrs round and round? The answer is that when light or heat is required we use bare electricity, whereas when power is required we keep the electricity covered up. The constant flow of sparks, unable to escape, is converted into energy. This energy is fed into a motor which makes things go round and round.

I have not yet touched on fuse wire. It has always amazed me that an industry which is so enterprising in most respects—the invention of colour electricity for use in traffic lights and the harnessing of negative electricity for refrigeration are two examples that come to mind—should still, two hundred years after James Watt invented the electric kettle, be manufacturing fuse wire too thin. I pass on a hint for what it is worth. There is available from hardware shops a sturdy wire used mostly for making chicken runs, and this is far more durable than the stuff sold by electricians (who must, I appreciate, make a living). By using chicken wire I now have a fuse box which—even when the spin-dryer burst into flames due to too much booster electricity having been fed into it—has for six months been as impregnable as the Bank of England.

But why have fuse wire at all? I completely understand that the fuse box is the junction at which the wires leading from the power station join, or fuse with, the wires belonging to the house, and that these two sets of wires have got to be connected with each other somehow. But what is wrong with a simple knot? Perhaps I might make this the subject of a paper for the *Electrical Journal* which, I now see from the *Writers' and Artists' Year Book*, welcomes electro-technical contributions not exceeding 3,000 words. In some respects, I reiterate, my knowledge is imperfect. I have not yet explored the field of neon signs—how do they make the electricity move about? And the pop-up toaster —how does it know when the toast is ready? With an electronic eye, presumably—and this brings us to another fruitful area. What is the difference between electricity and electronics? Or is there a difference? Is electronics now just the smart word to use, like high-speed gas? How can an English computer speak French, which requires a different voltage? Logic would answer these questions too, and many of a more technical nature, but the light over my desk has just gone out. A valve blown somewhere, I expect.

George Orwell and the postal system

A feature of English life is the large bookshop. There must be about thirty of these in London alone, and I have no doubt that there are others in the provinces. In appearance they are pretty much the same: a few shelves stacked with the latest novels, a table of war memoirs and biography, a department devoted to children's books and probably a basement festooned with the latest paperbacks (Penguin, Panther, Four Square etc. etc.).

In recent months most, if not all, of these shops have begun to stock certain red-coloured volumes perhaps two inches thick and weighing about half a pound each. (This is guesswork—I have no kitchen scales.) These books are usually displayed in sets of four. They are all volumes of the same work—the Collected Essays, Journalism and Letters of George Orwell. They cost £2.50p each, so that a set of four would cost roughly £10. The appeal of these books is clear. They are aimed at readers who, for one reason or another, want to own the Collected Essays, Journalism and Letters of George Orwell.

Who Orwell is I have no idea. The name is evidently a pseudonym, and probably he does not exist. It seems unlikely that a collection totalling 2,041 pages could be the work of the same person. Presumably Orwell is a trade name reserved by the publishers for this kind of thing.

Next to bubble-gum cards, these books of Orwell's give us probably the most reliable index to what is really important in England today. It is well worth getting hold of them and examining the contents. Discounting introductions, appendices and so on, the four books consist of five hundred and three items of differing lengths ranging from half a page to fifty-three pages. Putting aside various essays and other bits and pieces, they can be broken down in the following way:

Poems ...	...	...	4
Prefaces ...	...	...	4
Diaries ...	...	...	5
Book reviews	...	...	64
Letters ...	...	...	251

What is immediately plain is that there are four times as many letters as book reviews, and sixty-two times more letters than poems. Even if one includes the essays and bits and pieces, the letters still account for fractionally under fifty per cent of the total number of items. It is evidently as a letter-writer that Orwell has made his mark on the middle-class public—the journalists, lawyers, politicians, gentlemen farmers and the like who take in his stuff. His publishers would not think it worthwhile to charge £10 for the four volumes if this were not so. They know their market.

Orwell's style as a correspondent is no better and no worse than a score of others in the same *genre*. The following are fair samples:

Dear Cyril,
    I see from the N.S. & N. list that you have a book coming out sometime this spring. If you can manage to get a copy sent to me I'll review it.

Here is one to someone else:

Dear Spender,
    I hope things go well with you.

The first thing that anyone would notice about these letters is that they are private. The ones I have quoted are entirely typical. The familiarity 'Dear Cyril' is repeated over and over again, and so is 'Dear Dennis' (three times), 'Dear Tony' (ten) and 'My dear Runciman.' What the letters do is to satisfy the English weakness for reading other people's mail. It is ridiculous to suppose that this is not an English characteristic, especially of the upper middle class. It probably dates from the Penny Post Act of 1840. For the first time the common people, the servants, livery-men, stable-boys and others, were able to communicate with each other without fear of being overheard by Lord This or Lord That. The propertied classes have always misunderstood the danger to them of social change, and so they imagined that the threat would come from an organised Left. Fearing revolution, they began to read their servants' mail. Even a cursory glance at Victorian literature will show how the habit infiltrated down to the middle and lower middle classes. I can think off-hand of a score of cheap railway novels where the plot revolves on a letter falling into the wrong hands.

This explains the popularity of Orwell's letters, but it is important to ask another question, and that is why they were made public in the first place. After all, publishing is only a trade like any other, and Secker and Warburg (Orwell's publishers) could have made just as much money by putting out cheap reprints or pornography. There is one point about the Orwell letters that is significant—the date. They were published about the same time, probably even in the same month, as the two-tier postal system was introduced. It was vitally necessary for the Government to get the English masses 'letter-minded,' otherwise the two-tier scheme could not have worked. The release of the Orwell letters at this time was only a minor move, but it succeeded in getting the English people to think favourably about letters, and thus about the postal system. That presumably was the calculation.

Now it is absurd to deduce from this that there was any

collusion between Orwell, Secker and Warburg and the Postmaster-General. To call Orwell a government lackey is to suggest a sinister plot that simply does not exist. Secker and Warburg are, so far as I know, reputable men, and the Postmaster-General is at worst an ineffectual ass. There was no sinister plot. That is not how the English political system works. In this country it is enough for the ruling classes to make their wishes known, and men like Secker, Warburg and Orwell will *instinctively* do what is required of them. For what conceivable reason shouldn't they? I have no idea how much they make a year out of this letters business, but it must be a sizeable sum. It would be childish to expect them not to support the Post Office for all they are worth. There is a strong case for thinking that the system under which Orwell and Co. flourish should be altered. What there is no case for is to denounce Orwell and his like for behaving as they do. That is simply an example of British hypocrisy, and the sort of thing for which Europeans, who at any rate understand the function of the English postman, justifiably despise us.

In praise of supermarkets

Any urbane, reasoned essay in defence of supermarkets must, almost by definition, contain a good deal of material that might be considered libellous towards a snivelling, fawning, weevil-faced grocer called R. Sibson of The Stores, 14 High Street, Widsbury Green.

So I had better make it clear from the outset that R. Sibson is not his real name. His real name is G. Purbeck, and I have such a tale to tell of stale cheese and rancid butter, of body odours and dirty fingernails, of over-charging and weighted scales, of watered milk and sanded sugar, as would inspire any right-minded jury to march on The Stores and raze that rat-infested pavilion of incompetence to its beetle-ridden foundations. However, I have been advised by solicitors not to tell it. In fact, I have been advised by solicitors to keep constructive criticism of G. Purbeck down to the absolute minimum, notwithstanding that I was prepared to cloak his foul identity under the pseudonym of R. Sibson, telephone number Widsbury Green 342.

To the defence, then, of supermarkets.

I have never understood why they should incur the calumny of traditionalists, High Street conservationists, self-appointed arbiters of good taste or good living, or weevil-faced grocers rapidly approaching bankruptcy due solely to their reluctance to refund the price of a wrapped loaf that turned out to be green mouldy. It may well be true, as some of these critics argue, that supermarkets are somewhat soulless establishments, that the personal touch —as it might be a thumb-print on the Cheddar cheese— is missing, and that they are hygienic and free from body odours and rats to an almost fanatical degree.

Granting the force of these stupid arguments, we must set against them the advantages of the average supermarket over the typical grocer's shop with its snivelling proprietor, its cat asleep on the bacon slicer, its portrait of the Queen hiding the rising damp, and its short-sighted policy of not stocking Liversedge's ginger marmalade even when the demand is there.

There are, clearly, certain services which the super-market cannot and does not pretend to offer. It does not, for example, set itself up as an authority on the race meetings at Kempton Park. It does not instruct its cashiers to harangue customers on the need for strikers to be locked up and the country placed under the presidency of the Duke of Edinburgh. It does not keep fifteen people waiting while it recounts the exploits of its grandson Derek, aged three. Nor does it pretend to be a doctor, a meteorologist, a television critic, a gardening expert, or a judge of the morality of youth.

What the supermarket does have to offer is efficiency. The tinned anchovies are on the left as you go in and the potted meats are on the right as you come out. It is rarely, if ever, that you will catch the Messrs. Sainsbury peering vacantly into a drawer in the hope of locating either of these products. Nor do you often hear them telephoning their sister Maureen to inquire where she put the sardines while helping out last Saturday. And when did a prospec-tive customer last roll up at Tesco only to find the premises locked up and a pencilled note Sellotaped to the window regretting any inconvenience caused owing to the wedding of Miss M. Sibson or, for that matter, Miss M. Purbeck?

Some sociologists, as well as the occasional whining grocer jumping on the sociologists' band-wagon, express concern at the decline of the consumer's role in supermarket shopping. They postulate, either in their reports or in illiterate letters to the *Widsbury Green Mid-Weekly Bugle*, that the consumer falls easy prey to threepence-off gimickry and the lure of trading stamps, with the result that a whole generation is growing up which knows nothing of the economics of shopping.

There may be something in this, although what an older generation learned about the economics of shopping from a bill which not only added in the date but also charged them for a pound of lard that was never delivered is open to question. What is certainly true is that a whole generation is growing up which, when it requires a jar of Liversedge's ginger marmalade, has only got to steer a wire basket in the direction of the jams and preserves shelf. Whatever Victor Value or Safeways may lack in the way of the personal touch, they do not bar Liversedge's van-driver from coming near their premises on the grounds that he once kicked their grandson Derek, aged three, up the backside for giving him cheek. Neither, if Liversedge's ginger marmalade is out of stock, do they try to fob their customers off with a pound of treacle.

It is, come to think of it, the very absence of the personal element that, despite the drawbacks outlined above, gives the supermarket its slight edge over the tatty, broken-down, ill-lit, fusty, smelly, badly organised grocer's shop. Let me summarise the marginal advantages in an entirely hypothetical illustration. Imagine a High Street that is dominated by a well-equipped, spacious supermarket which for the sake of argument we will call Sainsbury's. A few doors further down is a condemned lock-up hovel owned by a smirking, sycophantic grocer whom we will call R. Sibson, or better still G. Purbeck.

Now supposing that I have a modest shopping list comprising half a pound of Normandy butter, a dozen standard eggs, a tin of cashew nuts and a jar of Liversedge's ginger marmalade.

The advantages of giving my custom to Sainsbury's are as follows:

1. My purchases are assembled without fuss from clearly labelled, adequately stocked shelves. The manager, if appealed to for some item that is not readily on view, does not stare at the ceiling muttering 'Cashew nuts, cashew nuts, cashew nuts' over and over again like a scratched gramophone record.

2. If the heir to the Sainsbury fortunes, aged three, took it into his head to juggle with my standard eggs, I could expect one of the senior Sainsburys to fetch him a clip over the ear. I would not expect to be charged for broken eggs.

3. It is, I believe, part of Sainsbury's policy not to snivel about the Common Market when selling Normandy butter.

The advantages in giving my custom to R. Sibson or G. Purbeck may be summarised in one word. Credit. Against this, however, one must set a profusion of libellous notices in the shop window, accusing certain customers of not having paid their bills.

On balance, it seems plain that the supermarket is here to stay while the familiar corner shop is destined either to be closed down by the public health authority or set on fire for the insurance money. I have no particular axe to grind but I cannot help feeling that, for once, progress is on the side of the consumer.

What do you mean, Splendide?

Q. Perhaps I am highly-strung or something, but every time I stay in a hotel I think I am about to have a nervous breakdown. This feeling is brought on by indifferent service, inefficient management and always being put over the ballroom. Should I hang myself instead of going on holiday this year?

A. *You do not say whether you are working to a budget. If expense is no object, why not take me along with you and book me into the next room, when my advice will be available at all reasonable hours?*

Q. Thank you. Here we are at the hotel, then, and as you have just heard with your own ears, my first problem is that they are full to the rafters and deny all knowledge of my advance booking.

A. *Luckily for us you have about your person a letter from the management, confirming the booking.*

Q. Actually, I haven't. It never arrived.

A. *Then for God's sake look as if it did arrive and stop sidling around the reception desk as if you were trying to get a room for Mr. and Mrs. Smith. Tell the manager that you are not interested in the problem he has been having with temporary personnel. Tell him that you would sooner slit your throat than stay in the alternative accommodation he suggests. Tell him the reason you refuse to produce the letter confirming the booking is that you may need it in evidence. All this will get you a reputation as a*

52

trouble-maker, and we will be given our rooms.

Q.   Here I am in my room but it does not have a bath, although I specified one in my booking.

A.   *Have you allowed the porter to dump your suitcase on a sort of large camp-stool with a canvas slatted top?*

Q.   Yes.

A.   *Did you tip him?*

Q.   Yes. Ten pence.

A.   *Then I am afraid that you have had it. You are welcome to have a bath in my room directly. Why my room has a bath and yours hasn't is that I refused point-blank to take possession of one lacking that elementary convenience. For that reason, you will find me in the bridal suite.*

Q.   Now we are in the Louis Quatorze Grill-room on the mezzanine, and they are refusing to give us anything to eat on the grounds that it is after 6.45 pm. Must we go hungry?

A.   *No. Quote the Innkeeper's Liability Act.*

Q.   But surely that is to do with lost luggage and so forth?

A.   *The Cypriot head waiter is not to know that. Just quote it. You may also tell him, in case he is thinking of doing anything unspeakable to the soup before wheeling it in, that I am the chief inspector of* The Good Food Guide.

Q.   We are having a few post-prandial brandies together in the residents' lounge and I am finding it increasingly difficult to attract the night porter's attention. Why is this?

A.   *This is because the night porter, like all night porters, is a puritan who thinks our monstrous licensing laws should not allow of any loophole for hotel residents. He will not bring us any more brandy until you make it clear that there will be an ugly scene otherwise.*

Q.   Here he comes now. Perhaps you could pay, since I have run out of money and it is your round.

A.   *Sign the bill.*

Q.   But the night porter says I may not sign the bill.

A.   *Give the night porter twenty-five pence and ask him*

*if you may borrow his pen. By the way, you might as well
make those doubles while you are about it.*

Q. Now I am up in my room and it is 2.15 am.

A. *Yes, I see it is. I did specify, you know, that my
advice was available at all reasonable hours.*

Q. I know, and that is the very point I want to take up.
There is a sort of cardboard pyramid on my dressing-table
with the printed information that room service operates
for twenty-four hours. I want a cheese sandwich.

A. *If you think I am going to make it for you, you must
be insane.*

Q. No, not you, *them.* I got through to the switchboard
after a delay of ten minutes, and they said they would ring
me back. That was half an hour ago. How long must I
wait?

A. *For ever, if you are going to swallow that particular
ploy. Ring the switchboard again and tell them—*

Q. That I want the night waiter immediately?

A. *Clearly you have not stayed in many hotels, or you
would know that the night waiter is supposed to be off
with 'flu. Ring the switchboard and dictate the following
telegram to the chairman of the group controlling this
hotel.* DEAR HENRY YOU LOSE YOUR BET STOP
WAS REFUSED CHEESE SANDWICH AT TWO FIF-
TEEN ACK EMMA REGARDS. *You then await results,
which should take five minutes.*

Q. The manager of the hotel is at my door with a cheese
sandwich garnished with watercress. Should I tip him?

A. *No. Go to sleep.*

Q. I am sorry to disturb you again, but it is now break-
fast-time. I have ordered fresh lemon juice—

A. *Fresh* lemon *juice? At this hour?*

Q. Yes, I am on a diet. Anyway, the waiter has just
brought me tinned lemon juice. I have told him that it
is tinned lemon juice but he swears that he has just
squeezed the lemon himself. I can hardly call him a liar,
can I?

A. *Is it the same fellow we had the barney with about dinner last night?*

Q. Yes. The one who said he would swing for you.

A. *What you do then is this. Produce a test tube from your pocket. Pour the lemon juice carefully into it, cork it, and make an inscrutable entry in a small black notebook. The fresh lemon juice will be brought to you personally by the chef, together with an explanation of there having been ze mistake in ze kitchen.*

Q. While packing, I have found another sort of cardboard pyramid which says the management regrets that bills cannot be settled by cheque. Owing to your having drunk all that brandy last night, I have not the cash to meet my commitments. Should we get out through the window?

A. *Certainly not. Send a little note to the management regretting that bills cannot be settled in cash. You will then pay by cheque and ask them what they propose to do about it.*

Q. One final question. I am being asked for fifteen per cent service charge. Should I tip the man who whistles up our cab?

A. *Of course not, have this one on me. I say, can you lend me five pence?*

To market, to market

Continental farmers, many from Common Market countries, are buying up agricultural land in Britain in an attempt to cash in on cheaper prices ...
—*Sunday Telegraph*

In well over half a century of contributing these *Rural Notes*, I have noticed many changes in our little valley. The curlew has disappeared and reappeared, the shire horse has given way to the ubiquitous tractor, conifers now grow in Folly Wood, and Orchard Farm (once part of the manor of Clogdale-by-Sumpbeck but now owned by my good friend Herr Doktor Heinrich von Scharnhorst) no longer dispenses shilling teas to the weary rambler. The weary rambler, truth to tell, would be put to the test to reach Orchard Farm at all nowadays, for there is barbed wire across the stile, and in recent summers Four Acre Meadow has been sown with detonators, steel traps and land-mines on the rotation principle. But those with eyes to see may still observe, from the floodlit watchtower by the Old Barn, the badger's dam on Sump Beck, just to the north of Dr Scharnhorst's submarine mooring. Now a year ago there were no badgers in this valley and, come to that, no magpies either; but now a pair of the cheeky rogues have built their nest not only in the watchtower but in the very machine-gun emplacement itself!

Townees often accuse us country folk of being resistant

to change. Not a bit of it. We are, when all's said and done, but the servants and hand-maidens of Mother Nature, and truly she is the ficklest of creatures who wears now her summer finery of green and gold, now the sombre rustling taffeta of autumn—and a moment later, nothing will do but that she must change into shimmering white, at once, for the Snow Ball. So we are used to innovation in our little valley.

Take swallow-shooting for example. Now I don't know how they order their affairs on the other side of Widow's Peak—for the village across the hill might be a million miles away for all we know of it—but we had never heard of swallow-shooting in Clogdale-by-Sumpbeck until last summer. Now, of course, it is all the go. No sooner has the first swooping migrant appeared over the spire of St. Bernadette-with-Childe than Old Dan and Jack and Bill and Karl and Henri abandon their tractors and reach for their guns, village lads and lasses pour out of the schoolroom and clamour for catapults at the tiny shop on the green, and Dr Scharnhorst polishes up his howitzer. M. Phillipe de Courvoisier, a local sheep-farmer whose land marches with the Martin Bormann estate, will pay up to fifty new pence for a brace of fat swallows; and if they do not end up in a fine crusty pie, to be served as the *pièce de résistance* at the village fete ('The Fiesta of a Hundred Saints,' as it is now known in the new-fangled lingo), then Mme de Courvoisier is not the cook she was.

But if one swallow does not make a summer, nor does a swallow pie make a social revolution. In all essentials, Clogdale-by-Sumpbeck is still the same huddle of crag and cottage that the monks of Cuthbert's Abbey must have espied from Widow's Peak as they traversed the wool road down to Shoddy Bottoms. If there is now a telephone box where the maypole used to stand, if the electric light has replaced the twinkle of oil-lamps in the shepherd's hovel, and electric fencing the drystone wall around Orchard Farm; and if guard dogs roam among Farmer Scharnhorst's apple trees, and Ye Olde Tea Shoppe is now

Le Bistro Ancien—why, it is only because your canny dalesman, with his eye to the main chance, is ever willing to take the best and reject the worst. Change we will tolerate, but not change for the sake of it. Thus and thus the butter cross stands on the green where it ever did; a scarecrow fashioned before the reign of Good Queen Victoria—aye, and still wearing his frock coat and chimney-pot hat —guards M. de Courvoisier's vineyard on the south side of the valley; and the old weather-vane turns yet on what is now the Clogdale-nächste-Sumpbeck Bierkeller Und Gymnasium.

Not all village folk would share my sanguine view of the way things are going of course—it would be a dull world if we all agreed. Only the other day I was enjoying a thimble or two of mazagran in the Black Bull with Old Moffat, a local pigman, and he, as is his wont, was full of complaints. 'T'owld village ent t'same,' he grumbled in his sturdy dialect. 'Ah'll gi' thee a jather (example). Ah wor bahn (bound) ower t'leea (common ground) t' to fetch mi creel (wood and rope farming implement used for carrying hay), an' ah'd just got past t' arrondisement speean (parish pump) when ah spied t' gauleiter (Farmer Scharnhorst).' And to Old Moffat's wemmle (surprise), Farmer Scharnhorst was drilling his sheep on the village green. The sight of this crack battalion of black-faced Rough Fell rams forming threes, slow-marching or moving briskly into open order for their morning inspection has been familiar enough for some time now, although not so familiar that old squaddies such as myself do not feel a thrill of pride when, to the strains of the Horstwessel over the Tannoy system which Dr Scharnhorst has kindly donated to the village, the sheep march smartly back to the fells for the spring manoeuvres; yet it is understandable that such as Old Moffat, who never left the valley during the late unpleasantness, should regard this quaint spectacle with gloppen (astonishment).

Yes, Old Moffat, stout fellow that you are, pigman among pigmen, salt of the earth, of course you are right—

't'owld village ent t'same'. Nowadays you must needs buy your drop of Pernod with 'new pence' instead of honest shillings; a stick of French bread, piping hot from Mme. Courvoisier's kitchen, costs twice as much and goes half as far as the old sliced loaf that the baker's van used to bring to the village before Dr Scharnhorst sealed off the road into Shoddy Bottoms; there are forms from the Department of Agriculture to be wrestled with before a man may nail his geese to the floor to fatten them up for Pâté de Foie du Clogdale-par-Sumpbeck, our local delicacy; very soon, if Whitehall gets its way, our fields of sauerkraut will be measured by the hectare and not by the acre.

And yet, and yet! Do we not still hear the cheery song of the chaffinch hard by Bormann's Field, and are those not trout that jump as if electrocuted where the rippling beck passes through Scharnhorst's farm? Stands the church clock at fourteen fifty hours, and is there wiener schnitzel still for tea?

Blood money

The Government should order doctors to stop over-prescribing rather than introduce complicated new prescription charges if it wants to cut the cost of medicines, leading chemists said today

—*Daily Telegraph*

Young Shirley Neverwell was worried about her complexion, as well she might have been. She was a deep yellow in hue, which was leading her workmates to call her Buttercup.

'Still at the match factory?' I asked. 'I thought so. You've got phossy jaw.'

'That's what old Dr. Goodenough used to tell me,' volunteered Shirley. 'He always used to prescribe copper sulphate ($1\frac{1}{2}$-3 grains) as an emetic.'

'Yes, well I'm afraid those days are over, Shirley,' I said. 'Do you know how much copper sulphate is fetching per ton on the open market? Stick your finger down your throat, there's a good girl. And for God's sake go and get a job in Woolworth's.'

Neville Heath Neverwell is one of my regulars. Hardly an evening surgery goes by without he doesn't pop in complaining of some little ache and pain or other. This time it was haemoglobinuria, jaundice, fever, vomiting, and severe haemolysis.

'Spleen and liver enlarged, are they?' I asked. 'Epigastric discomfort? Passing port-wine-coloured urine?'

Neville nodded.

'I thought as much,' I said. 'Blackwater fever.'

The old-fashioned treatment for Neville's trouble is absolute rest, plenty of alkaline fluids, blood transfusion, and glucose given intravenously. But I thought I'd try a little experiment.

'Here's a prescription for a bottle of Lucofizz on sale or return,' I said. 'Take three tablespoons a day and try to keep out of draughts, Central Africa, India and the Far East.'

That was four weeks ago and Neville hasn't been back since. Either blackwater fever has taken its toll or he's pocketed the threepence back on the Lucofizz bottle, which of course by rights belongs to the National Health.

Lady Eleanor de Gray Beaufort Neverwell wasn't too put out when her youngest, the Hon. Cedric, swallowed a new penny. He's a rare one for sucking coins of the realm, and over the years he has acquired something of a local reputation as a walking piggy-bank.

'Old Dr. Goodenough believed in nature taking its course,' confided Lady E. 'As a general rule he would recommend a little syrup of figs to help things along.'

'Figs,' I had to tell her, 'do not grow on trees. I shall have to operate. How much currency is within the little shaver as of even date?'

'About 25p, some of it in old money,' she reported.

'Finders keepers,' I said.

For as long as I've been in practice Francisco de Isturiz Neverwell, SJ, has been asking for what we in the medical profession call a bunch of fives.

He suffers, you see, from digital poisoning, which is brought on by taking medicine in excessive doses. Francisco's heartbeat was slow and irregular, he had been having convulsions, and he was, at the time he was wheeled into into my surgery on a handcart, unconscious.

All this was brought on by swigging, in vast quantities, weak potassium permanganate solution which is supposed to be the remedy for the very complaint I have just described.

'You're in a vicious circle, Francisco, lad,' I advised him. burning a few feathers under his nose. 'You do realise, I hope, that the leading chemists have got up a petition against you and your extravagant ways?'

'Old Dr. Goodenough,' he gasped, 'used to give me blank prescription forms and leave me to fill them in myself.'

'You know perfectly well,' I replied, 'that old Dr. Goodenough has just been struck off for over-prescribing liniment of camphor to immigrants who use it as a basis for a very dry cocktail. I'm giving you two aspirins and I want you to suck them, not crunch them.'

I had to climb on my high horse when Queen Juliana Neverwell, who suffers from hereditary microcytic hypochromic anaemia, dropped into the surgery.

'Brittle nails you may have as a result of your condition,' I exploded. 'But if you think you are getting Revlon Crystalline Spunsugar Pink nail varnish on prescription, thus placing leading chemists in the embarrassing position of having to rat on their superior colleagues, you have got to be out of your skull. And furthermore,' I went on, 'there is enough preparation of ferrous sulphate left in this bottle to keep a family of five on 200 to 400 mg thrice daily for the rest of their lives. Kindly get out of my sight.'

Glubb Pasha Neverwell of that Ilk is a martyr to nervous diseases. Since my Black's Medical Dictionary was due back at the public library shortly before he dropped in to see me, I was unable to pinpoint his symptoms more closely than that.

I do know, however, that old Dr. Goodenough was a fool to himself in prescribing phenobarbitone sodium, allobarbitone, butobarbitone, amylobarbitone, pentobarbitone, cyclobarbitone, hexobarbitone, quinalbarbitone and headache powders in quantities sufficient to make it worth young Neverwell's while to have them carted away in a lorry.

'I'm putting you on Pontefract Castle Toffee Assortment, Glubb,' I explained. I didn't bother to tell him that these are what we medicoes call a placebo; they're available from all reputable confectioners at 10p a quarter, and if they don't keep you out of the dentist's at least they keep you out of the leading chemists, except for an emergency issue of cotton-wool soaked in a mixture of chloral and menthol. which is nothing whatever to do with me.

The Rt. Hon. Plantagenet Berkeley Arbuthnot Neverwell, Pretender to the Ancient Throne of Wessex, is a bit of a malingerer between you and me. He does in fact have a touch of coal miner's lung, Kümmell's Disease, gout, fatty degeneration of the heart, paralysis of the abducent nerve, hernia, misplaced sternum, St. Anthony's Fire, neurasthenia, Mediterranean fever, gall-stones, dyspepsia, ringworm of the beard, mushroom poisoning, simple enlargement of the thyroid gland, lead colic, bromidrosis, impetigo, botulism and chapped hands, but as I keep telling him, so who's perfect?

'You're a good customer, Plantagenet,' I said, 'and I'm offering you first lick of the spoon that old Mrs. Wilkinson, God rest her soul, has been using for her liver extract.'

'No deal,' he replied, all hoity-toity. 'When old Dr. Goodenough was here it was out with the trade samples from ICI, Boots, all the big names—one month's prescription on approval, perm any five from six.'

'We live in changing times,' I told him. 'Let's save the taxpayer a few bob and put you on Frenkel's Exercises, to be performed by patients having difficulty in controlling their muscles.'

'But I need medicine, doctor! There's nothing wrong with my muscles.'

'There will be,' I said, 'if you don't get out of here and stop wasting public money.'

By bread alone

You wake up late as usual. You stagger into the kitchen with only five minutes to prepare a scratch breakfast. And your nostrils are assailed by the smell of hot buttered toast and fresh coffee.

Yet you have no maid. No wife either. You are not staying in a hotel, and you are not dreaming.

The bread has toasted itself.

Not only that. It has made the coffee, squeezed an orange, fetched in the morning papers, vacuumed the living room and answered your routine mail.

Fantastic?

Ridiculous?

An Alice-in-Wonderland Utopia? Or just another boffin's-eye-view of the shape of things to come in 1984?

Not at all.

It is happening.

It is fact.

Automated bread is here NOW.

In England, it's true, it is not yet on public sale. But in Southern California Mrs. American Housewife can go to her Supermarket TODAY and buy a loaf of bread that will not only arrange itself into triangular sandwiches but will ring up her friends to invite them to a bridge party. Soon, according to the *Scientific American*, the housewife won't even have to leave her home to get her automated bread. Merely by inserting a credit-card through a mag-

64

netic slot on her kitchen wall she will be able to summon a loaf of bread that will make its own way to her door by public transport or, for 50 pence extra, by Yellow Cab.

How does automated bread work?

The secret is in tiny computerised memory cells, the size of a crumb, which are inserted into each slice. These crumbs—they are edible, with a slightly bitter taste—can be programmed to do anything required of them. So that a loaf of pumpernickel may leave the bakery not only ready to be made into pastrami sandwiches but equipped—should the customer so wish it—for a career in the garment trade.

'After the assembly line, the bread line,' said *Time* magazine, announcing this new industrial revolution.

In America today automated bread is replacing the traditional coloured maid in thousands of homes.

A soft roll in Orange County, California, is often left in sole charge of five children.

A wholemeal loaf in Swollen Jaw, Arizona, helps to run a secretarial college.

And by 1975, according to the *American Scientist,* a bag of Italian breadsticks may be running for Governor in New York State.

And here in Britain?

A spokesman for the Allied Electronic Bread Laboratory in Stevenage said:

'Frankly, we have lost out to the United States on this one. We could bring out automated bread tomorrow but in view of the Americans' head start it would sell only on the home market. We have got to think of exports.

'So we are thinking in terms of a computerised muffin. By storing the memory-cell in currants we will be able to turn out a more versatile yet lighter product. Pretty soon we expect to be bombarding the States with a muffin that will sing an old English folk song while you butter it.

'You may also be interested in the fact that I am a Marie Louise biscuit.'

What started the automated bread race?

American know-how, naturally.

In 1963 the American Electronics Corporation—now taken over by the Electronics Corporation of America—acquired a controlling interest in The House of a Million Doughnuts, previously owned by a computer firm which it had itself just taken over. The House of a Million Doughnuts was a nation-wide chain of bakery outlets which had not changed its policy—'Smell 'em! They're so Mmmmmmm!'—since making a fortune for a Dutch immigrant in the nineteen-twenties.

A spokesman for the Corporation said:

'The trouble was, we were fighting guys who knew a whole lot more about the bread field than we did.

'They'd had years to develop a loaf that was tasteless and odourless. Motivational research, as well as the balance sheet, told them that this was what the customer wanted.

'We moved in new plant, got the flavour out of our product and caught up with our rivals. Then we introduced poly-stryuropopopopolene packaging, which keeps a loaf fresh—or at least edible—for six months. For a while we were ahead.

'Our competitors answered back with the infra-red loaf which stays edible for a year. Between us we'd taken bread just as far as it would go—as bread.

'That's when we decided to go all out for the automated loaf market.'

And here's where Britain enters the story. For automated bread was a *British* invention. In 1962 a West country scientist had inserted a primitive battery into a Cornish scone and watched fascinated while it shampooed his carpet.

But British manufacturers were not interested. He joined the brain drain.

In his suitcase as he touched down at Kennedy International Airport?

The first automated loaf.

With American backing, punch-card Passover bread and a low-calory crispy biscuit that beats as it sweeps as it cleans were soon on public sale. Encouraged, the back-room boffins began to experiment on a cracked-wheat loaf that could receive high frequency radio messages. The result of that experiment? Next year the Americans may launch the first teacake in space.

Other scientific uses of automated bread:

IT CAN keep a watch on tooth decay and warn young-sters when to see a dentist.

IT CAN—by emitting a high-pitched whistle audible only to police computers—warn of burglaries and fire.

IT CAN—by being programmed to bake itself—release thousands of men for more essential work.

IT MAY do the job of nurses—and, eventually, even brain surgeons—in understaffed hospitals.

But what about the ordinary housewife?

Does she *want* automated bread—which costs, incident-ally, three times more than the orthodox product?

The American Electronics spokesman said:

'She sure as hell wants progress, if that's what you mean. Remember, we're in a race with Moscow on this. Privileged party members in Russia can buy magnetically treated black bread that teaches them English while they sleep. God knows what's happening in China.

'Our job is to get ahead and stay ahead of the Com-munists. The White House is with us all the way down the line.'

If the Americans have the problem of keeping ahead of the Russians, our headache is keeping up with the Ameri-cans. At Consolidated Bread Products HQ in Lancashire, a high-level chip butty said:

'The question is one of capital investment. If the Govern-ment would give us the green light we could produce a loaf that would put us right in front in the bread race.

'As it is, we have to limit ourselves to novelty Eccles Cakes that say "Eeh bah gum" when you bite into them. We want more than pats on the back for our initiative—we want active Treasury support.'

Meanwhile food manufacturers on both sides of the

Atlantic are taking their cue from the automated bread revolution. Transistorised broiler chickens, magnetic apples and radio-active beef are all in the pipeline.

Is it all worth while?

As a Norwich poultry farmer—about to become a millionaire by switching to computerised turkeys—put it:

'For us, yes.'

Are you receiving me?

The Post Office and I differ on the way to handle a telephone. 'Answer your telephone promptly, giving your name, the name of your firm and your number,' I am advised in Chapter Fourteen of the A—D directory ('How to get the best from your telephone.') 'If when you pick up the telephone you hear a series of rapid pips, the call will be from a coinbox telephone. You must then wait for the caller to insert the money ...'

I can't be doing with that at all. If my telephone is to give of its best, it had better start by realising who is the boss around here. I am certainly not going to hang about dripping wet (not that I am likely to be dripping wet: the phone that rings when I am in the bath may continue to ring until I am out of it) while my coinbox callers fumble for their twopenny pieces. I am more likely to hang up, and were I the Post Office I would give the same advice to all subscribers. If when you pick up the telephone you hear a series of rapid pips, the call will either be from someone who wants to borrow money (a process known as wiretapping), or from a drunken friend who has just left the wife and is on the cadge for a meal, a bed and sympathy.

As for answering the telephone promptly, this counsel fails to recognise that nearly all phone calls are bad news. Whether preceded by a series of rapid pips or not, they are almost certain to be from people who want you to give them something or who want you to do something for them. I try to allow a good five minutes before answer-

ing the telephone, in the hope that my caller will turn to
the next subscriber on his list of suckers. Under no circumstances do I give my name, the name of my firm or
my number. After all, one does not roll up one's trouser leg
and show a mad dog the best place to bite. So:

'Hello?'

'Hello?'

'Hello?'

'What number is that?'

'It depends. What number do you want?'

'I was ringing the Marie Antoinette Wig Boutique.'

'Ah. This isn't it.'

'What number are you, then?'

'I am sorry, madam, but we have not been introduced,
and I cannot bandy personal digits with a complete stranger.'

Or, in the highly remote event of my caller not getting
the wrong number:

'Hello?'

'Hello?'

'Hello?'

(This gambit—strongly discouraged by the Post Office:
though why, since it must make them thousands, I cannot
imagine—is strongly recommended. Often, the trouble-
maker at the other end of the line will assume he is talking
to the family parrot, and hang up.)

'Hello!'

'Hello.'

'Is that Mr. Keith Waterhouse's number?'

'Supposing it was, and I'm not admitting that it is, why
do you want to know?'

*'I have the Inland Revenue on the line for Mr. Keith
Waterhouse.'*

'This is an answering machine speaking. It does not
know where Mr. Waterhouse is or when he will be back,
if at all. He may be dead. Will you please speak into the
tax-deductible tape recorder. You have three seconds in
which to record your message ...'

Or, in the even more highly remote event of it being a wet evening when the TV isn't working, there's nothing to read, I've just discovered that the patience deck has only 51 cards, I have an overdraft at the bank, and someone who might want to pay me money is on the phone—or at least in its near vicinity:

'Hello?'

'Hello?'

'Hello?'

'Is that Mr. Waterhouse?'

'I'm not sure. Who wants him?'

'I have the Editor of the New York Steam Laundry Daily Leisure Supplement for you, Mr. Waterhouse. Hold on, please.'

'No, no, *you* hold on, please. If you had the Editor of the New York Steam Laundry Daily Leisure Supplement for me, he'd be holding on for me, rather than the other way round. What you mean, surely, is that you have me—assuming it is me, and you would have to take my word for that, which cannot be trusted—for the Editor of the New York Steam Laundry Daily Leisure Supplement?'

'I'm putting you through now.'

But you're not, dear Lady, because I've hung up.

'Hello?'

'Hello, caller. What number are you please?'

'I think there's some confusion in your mind. You just rang my telephone and I, since I was passing by at the time, answered it. This makes you the caller, not me.'

'What number are you please?'

'Well, since you put that question to me, I'm not a number at all: I'm a living, being, human entity. If you prick me, do I not bleed? If you tickle me, do I not laugh? If you poison me—'

'Is that Mr. Waterhouse?'

'It could be, in certain circumstances.'

'I have the Editor of the New York Steam Laundry Daily Leisure Supplement for you, Mr. Waterhouse. I believe we were cut off.'

71

'No, we weren't cut off. I had some things to do, so I put the receiver back on its hook.'

Now you may argue, if you will, that the respondent in the above conversation, who may or may not have been my good self (that we shall never know because, since I haven't given my number or admitted to my name, I could just as easily be Alan Brien talking through a handkerchief and pretending to be Alan Coren) is rude, evasive, pedantic, overbearing, unhelpful, and possibly that he has the mind of a child of five. What you cannot deny, however, is that he is thoroughly enjoying himself. Enjoined by the Post Office to get the best out of his telephone, he does so by employing it as a weapon, wielding his two-tone handset as, in the gymnasium, he would wield a foil or épée—that is to say, like a meat-axe.

In real life our man is diffident to the point of cowardice, polite to the point of sycophancy, tolerant to the point of listening to long jokes which he has already heard. But telephone life is not real life—you can tell that by the way professional telephonists talk, which is as if they had been to a finishing school for Daleks. Telephone life is dream life, fantasy life, Walter Mitty life, and when our man's blower rings it might just as well be a party call for Ali Khan, Mad Mitch, the United States Marines and—'Hello? Hello? Hello?'—Dixon of Dock Green.

His telephone is an ego-bolsterer, a watchdog at the threshold of his privacy, a deflater of pomp, a rapier, a bludgeon and—in a conversation we have not yet been privileged to overhear—an offensive weapon such as, if it were to be carried about the streets at night, would be confiscated by the police and lay our man open to a six-months' sentence:

'*Inland Revenue.*'

'Hello?'

'*Inland Revenue. Whom did you wish to speak to?*'

'A certain R.D.M. oblique a lot of numbers, who claims to be my obedient servant.'

'*That would be Mr. McCorcodale. I'm sorry, caller, but Mr. McCorcodale is on annual leave.*'

'I thought he might be. Would you tell Mr. McCorcodale when he returns from his annual leave, that Waterhouse is spelt with one T, that he had better go through his innumerable files and re-discover my correct address, that the tax he is demanding would be consistent with an income of eighty thousand pounds a year, that his threats of legal action cut no ice whatever, and that if Mr. McCorcodale's accuracy with figures may be fairly judged by his pathetic attempts to get my postal code number right for once in his life, I shall look forward keenly to discussing the matter further in the High Court and if necessary the House of Lords.'

The only circumstances in which you can hold a conversation like that is on the telephone, when Mr. McCorcodale is on annual leave, and when you have written it all out beforehand.

A—Z of photography

APERTURE. A little hole in the camera through which a wife, child, dog, cat pawing a ball of wool, wedding, swan, Norman church, father up to his neck in sand, interesting old alley, sailor sticking his head out of a porthole, or Midlands couple who were the life and soul of the party that last night in Ibiza, may be observed by the photographer. At one time, due to a fault in the mechanism, these subjects appeared upside-down. Now the camera has been juggled about with so that they are now right way up, although this does not help as regards remembering the identity of that Midlands couple in Ibiza.

BOX BROWNIE. The photographic equivalent of the Model-T Ford. The Box Brownie comes in a sort of miniature gas-mask case, which makes it all the more suitable for taking the kind of nostalgic snap that, even on the day it comes back from the developers, makes all the women look as if their dresses are six inches too long.

CAMERA. An incredibly simple device for taking still pictures without batteries or plugs, unlike movie cameras which need either or both in order to make a whirring noise. The camera consists of a lens, a shutter, a button, an aperture to look at things through, some film and a red transparent disc with numbers on it. (See RED TRANSPARENT DISC WITH NUMBERS ON IT.) Jumbled up with all this gear are some other items too complex to explain, hence the camera's original name, Camera Obscura.

DEVELOPER. Some stuff which is smeared on the negative (see NEGATIVE) to turn it into a positive (see POSITIVE). This stuff is a chemical which turns black into white and white into black. Why the camera cannot be adapted to do this job itself, in the same way as it has been adapted to stop showing things upside down, has never been disclosed.

ENLARGEMENT. A means of making a photograph bigger by sending it off with a postal order to a firm of chemists.

FILM. The material on which precious fleeting moments are captured for all time. Originally, when photographers were in the habit of putting a bag over their heads before taking a picture, this film was made of glass. When photographers stopped putting bags over their heads and began to roam about using Box Brownies, it was found that glass was not malleable enough to roll up inside the new portable cameras. Hence celluloid, being less brittle, came into common use. It is not known why the precious fleeting moments cannot be captured for all time on a roll of Sellotape.

GODDARD, JOHN FREDERICK. The man who discovered in 1840 that if plates were sensitised with the vapour of bromine as well as iodine, it would lay the way open for John Frederick Goddard to get himself written up in reference books as the father of portrait photography. This also explains why all the subjects of early photography look as if they have just caught a whiff of vapour of bromine as well as iodine.

HIGH-SPEED FILM. It is generally known that when someone moves in a photograph, you get a sort of blur. With high-speed film, you do not get a sort of blur. This would seem to suggest that it is not high-speed film at all, since it seems to be fractionally behind what is going on at the time. However, that is the misnomer by which it is known in the trade.

INCIDENT LIGHT EXPOSURE READING.   A technical term used in manuals purporting to explain the art of photography to the layman.

JOULE CAPACITY OF FLASH UNITS.   An even more technical term used in the same manuals, which at this stage in the alphabet have lost their audience.

KODACHROME.   A proprietary colour film first introduced in 1936 for 35 mm still cameras. How colour film differs from black and white film is fascinating and remarkably easy to understand, but unfortunately the Kodachrome process, being proprietary, is copyright and therefore top secret.

LIGHT METER.   Somewhat like a traffic meter, it has an arrow which goes up to some high numbers when there is too much light, and down to the low numbers when there is not enough. Experienced photographers find that somewhere around the middle is just about right. You do not have to put any money in a light meter, by the way.

MAGIC.   The process by which someone can press a button and then fiddle around with the back of the camera, and out comes a finished print. Also known as Polaroid.

NEGATIVE.   A piece of film that makes everyone look like the Black and White Minstrel Show. Very interesting when held up to the light.

OVER-EXPOSURE.   An over-exposed photograph is one that makes its subjects look as if they have somehow acquired a deep sun-tan in the middle of a thunderstorm. Over-exposure is caused by leaving the camera switched on for too long. There are tables of numbers to help you over this problem, but if you think of your camera as a gas-cooker and of your subject as a pan of milk that is about to boil over, you cannot go far wrong.

POSITIVE. A snap, or more usually a series of snaps, contained in a yellow paper wallet. Some of these snaps have pictures on them and others are just black all over. The ones that are black all over have been over-developed by the stupid chemist and may be discarded.

QUIGLEY, GEORGE. A beach photographer on Southend Pier.

RED TRANSPARENT DISC WITH NUMBERS ON IT. This is the most important bit of gadgetry in the modern camera. Every time you take a picture, you must twist a sort of roller thing so that the number under the red transparent disc goes up by one. If it goes up by two, it probably means that you have got sand in your lens. When you get to number eight, it is time to put another roll of film in the camera, although it often turns out that it would have been quite safe to go on rolling until you had reached number sixteen.

SHUTTER. What comes down when you have taken a photograph. The shutter chops up your roll of film into separate pictures and thus prevents it from becoming a home movie.

TRIPOD. A three-legged stand on which big cameras may be mounted in order to prevent sand getting in the lens.

UNDER-EXPOSURE. The opposite of over-exposure. If you are still thinking of your camera as a gas-cooker, what you will get with under-exposure is the photographic equivalent of a lightly-boiled egg.

VILTAGE CONTROL. A misprint sometimes found in simple manuals for the novice photographer. What they mean is voltage control.

WAINWRIGHT, MRS. An early manufacturer of dry photographic plates who used to coat them by hand from a batch of emulsion prepared in a teapot. This side of the business was considerably expanded by Eastman Kodak, a worldwide enterprise involving millions and millions of teapots.

X-RAY. A spectacular photographic effect produced when electrons, accelerated to a very high speed in a vacuum by applying a high voltage, are allowed to impinge on a solid target such as a trouser-button swallowed by the baby.

Y-1/607D. The kind of name now being given to cameras in order to humiliate people who only know how to ask for a Box Brownie, and who wish they were dead.

Z. A letter of the alphabet which according to the leading manuals does not seem to be connected with photography in the slightest degree.

Liquorish allsorts

In a learned consideration of what it calls Ordinary Drunkenness, *Black's Medical Dictionary* remarks that 'it is too common to need much description.' Fortunately for any abstemious G.P. who might have trouble diagnosing the strange Oriental disease that causes strong men to cry, giggle or offer to fight any man in the surgery, *Black's Medical Dictionary* then has second thoughts and goes on to describe Ordinary Drunkenness in full, and with customary relish.

'First the person is brightened, his spirits rise, his conversation is witty, the skin becomes flushed, and there is a general sense of well-being.'

Leaving generalisations behind, Black then splits Ordinary Drunks into four categories. 'One person becomes angry, resents fancied affronts, and tries to pick quarrels; another becomes melancholy and lugubrious; a third grows maudlin, and weepingly recounts the secrets of his family to perfect strangers; while a fourth type assumes a regal manner and gives away his money and valuables or makes promises which he cannot possibly fulfil.'

So to summarise, it seems that we have Drunks A, B, C and D. Drunk A, the angry one, Drunk B, known to his friends as 'Melancholy Baby,' Drunk C, who cries in his beer, and Drunk D, with his overdraft and his delusions of grandeur.

Now as far as A, B and C are concerned, Black is on firm ground and he has given us some pretty shrewd thumbnail sketches of their behaviour when pie-eyed. They all happen to be close friends of mine and I have noticed the same symptoms myself. But what about this improbable chap D, flinging his money about and making wild promises? Here, I suggest, Black has let his imagination run away with him. In a long experience of stumbling across drunks, and sometimes over them, I have never stumbled across or over a drunk even remotely resembling the mysterious D.

I said as much to my friends A, B and C when, happening to run into them casually in the Dog and Boot the other night, I carried them off for a champagne supper at the Savoy Grill.

'I've been hearing,' I said, once the caviar had been ordered, 'about a rather amusing character called D. Drinks a bit, assumes a regal manner, gives away all his money and valuables. I wondered if any of you had come across him in your travels.'

B and C did not reply. B was moodily toying with the gold wristwatch, a memento of my late father, which I had given to him in the pub earlier. C was weeping quietly into his pheasant soup. It was A who spoke, knocking his chair over as he rose unsteadily to his feet.

'Come outside!' he said thickly.

'But my dear A! All I said was—'

'I heard what you said, you cross-eyed, bat-brained, stinking conchy! Come outside and repeat it, and I'll knock your yellow teeth down your lying throat! And as for your bloody platinum cigarette case,' he shouted throwing my little present back in my face, 'you can stuff it!'

'Oh, now look here, A, aren't you being a little hasty? Sit down, have a ten-pound note, and let's talk this thing over quietly.'

But A, kicking aside our wine waiter and upsetting his tray of champagne cocktails, had gone. I apologised to the rather nice people at the next table, for whom I had ordered the drinks, and snapped my fingers for another round.

'Rum chap, old A,' I said to my other two guests. 'Why should he get so upset, just because I asked him if he knew anyone called D?'

'Perhaps the name reminded him of something he'd rather forget,' said B mournfully. 'I know that's the effect it had on me.'

'You know D then, do you?' I asked eagerly, motioning to the waiter to fetch B a box of cigars. 'Is it true that he chucks his money about and makes promises which he cannot possibly fulfil?'

'I don't know him at all,' said B. 'But when you spoke about his money, it reminded me that if business doesn't pick up pretty soon, I shall probably have to go bankrupt in about twenty-five years.'

'Never fear, B,' I said. 'I will come to your rescue and underwrite your debts.'

'It's too late for that,' moaned B. 'No one can help me, no one, do you hear me, no one! I perceive,' he added, 'that we are quite close to the river. I might just as well nip across and throw myself in it.'

B departed. There was a silence, broken only by a splash from the other side of the embankment and the sound of C's sobbing. I helped my remaining guest to a boar's head with an apple in its mouth, ordered another magnum of champagne, and tried to comfort him.

'If it's any help, C,' I said, 'it does so happen that if I hadn't royal blood in my veins I would have become a qualified psychiatrist. Is there anything I can do?'

C, woebegone, shook his head. 'What a happy fellow this D must be!' he wailed at length. 'I don't suppose *his* wife is frigid and taunts him with being a failure! Oh, no! *Or* that his seventeen-year-old daughter has had three abortions in the last twelve months. And you do realise,' continued C, dabbing his eyes and blowing his nose vigorously, 'that my youngest son is a confirmed homosexual?'

'Poor old chap,' I said, patting his shoulder. 'I must see what I can do for you.'

'Do you mind?' said C with great dignity. 'This happens

to be a private conversation between me and the gentleman at the next table.'

He left shortly after that, to tell the cloakroom attendant about his father having been guilty of moral cowardice during the war. I was left by myself. I snapped my fingers and summoned three or four waiters.

'Sit down, waiters, and join me at dinner,' I said. 'I am shortly opening a new Mayfair restaurant, and I would like you to be my advisers in return for a substantial share of the profits. But first, I am anxious to trace the whereabouts of a fellow calling himself D. Rather fond of the fruit-juice, I believe, assumes a regal manner, gives away his money and valuables, makes promises which he cannot possibly fulfil. Tell me, does he come in here at all?'

'Not to the best of my knowledge, sir,' replied the head waiter, signalling to his minions to pick up the loose silver which I had thrown on the floor for them.

'I thought not,' I said, rising and signing the bill with a flourish. 'If he should by any chance come in, calling himself Black and claiming to be the publisher of a Medical Dictionary, you might just tell him from me he's barking up the wrong tree, would you?'

3. The light that failed

Looking for an orgy

I, Charles Septimus Parkin of 23A Jubilee Mansions, Norwood, make this statement voluntarily in the presence of Detective-Sergeant William Cooney and PC Throstle of 'E' Division. I am forty-three years old and a clerk in the employ of British Fat Products Ltd. I am married in name only. I do not wish to add to that.

I first became aware of the permissive society on or about September 5 1969. I remember the date because it is the birthday of my niece Avril, and I had bought her a Kooky-doll as a present. I do not know why the Kooky-doll is still in my possession, or why she was in the cistern cupboard. I cannot explain why she is wearing fish-net tights, see-through bra and a PVC mackintosh instead of the après-ski outfit depicted on her box. The Action Man produced by Det.-Sgt. Cooney from the cistern cupboard in my presence does not belong to me. I do not know why Action Man is wearing only his boots. The Polaroid camera is for the purpose of taking holiday snaps. The photograph which I ate before being cautioned by Det.-Sgt. Cooney was a holiday snap.

On or about September 5 1969 I read in a Sunday newspaper about a wife-swapping ring in Mauncey Road, Birmingham, together with an exposé of certain magazines 'for swingers only,' also photographs allegedly taken at a drug party in Leeds before the reporter made an excuse and left. It is not true that from that day on I became

85

obsessed by the permissive society, although what I read was certainly an eye-opener. I did not suggest to my wife Noreen that we should engage in similar activities. The phrase, 'Let's get some fun out of life while we're still young, or are you too frigid?' is not one that I would normally use. I did not place an advertisement in the *Swapper's Digest*. I have never heard of the *Swapper's Digest*.

I now recall that I did place an advertisement in the *Swapper's Digest*. The fifteen back numbers of this publication under the towels in the airing cupboard are for my own use. The advertisement was a joke. It has been put to me that 'Virile husband-and-wife duo wish to meet AC-DC couples, no prudes' does not sound like a joke, but I do not agree. It was an exercise in parody. I know nothing about an accommodation address in Soho. I received no replies to my advertisement.

I have never been in Mauncey Road, Birmingham.

I now recollect that I went to Mauncey Road, Birmingham, on September 9 and spoke to a woman now known to me as WPC Hawkins. My purpose in journeying to Birmingham was to visit an old army friend, 586 Cadger McNally, whose address I cannot at present remember. I asked WPC Hawkins to direct me to New Street Station. I did not employ any words such as 'Are you a swinger?' I recall employing the phrase, 'Where is the action?' This is an idiomatic expression indicating that I was looking for New Street Station.

I did not deposit a suitcase in the left-luggage office at New Street Station. I identify a suitcase produced by Det.-Sgt. Cooney as my property. I confirm that it did not fly to Birmingham of its own volition. The mask, riding-crop and length of rope are all my property. I purchased the mask at a novelty shop in Paddington in case my friend 586 Cadger McNally was giving his annual fancy-dress party. The riding-crop was a present for my married niece June, who is a keen horsewoman. I have no recollection whatsoever of proposing to my married niece June that I should be her gee-gee and that she should ride me around her living room. The length of rope was in case of fire. I have always carried a length of rope in case of fire ever since reading that Hans Christian Andersen did likewise. It has been put to me that Hans Christian Andersen is the same 'Fancypants' Andersen who is now doing bird at the Scrubs for thieving lingerie off of clothes lines. To the best of my knowledge Hans Christian Andersen was a writer of fairy tales. I have been informed what the expression 'fairy' means in common parlance. I have never been that way inclined. I have never been to Hampstead Heath.

It is not true that I was wandering about Leeds in a polka-dot dress and steel-blue nylon stockings on the night of September 9-10. The polka-dot dress produced by Det.-Sgt. Cooney was purchased at Selfridge's for my friend 586 Cadger McNally's fancy-dress party. I regard flushing clothes down the lavatory as a normal method of disposing of unwanted property.

Having been shown certain photographs, I now wish to correct any suggestion I may have made that I was not wandering about Leeds on the night of September 9-10, but I deny that I was looking for a so-called drag party. I was in Leeds for the simple reason that I got on the wrong train at Birmingham New Street Station. I was suffering from flu and had taken some tablets shortly before drinking a glass of beer. This must have made me light-headed. I was definitely not wearing the polka-dot dress, except for a short period.

I admit to having knocked at a door in Victoria Hospital Avenue, Leeds, between 12.30 and 12.45 am. I deny asking the lady now known to me as Mrs. Jeanette Henderson if there was room for one more. I deny suggesting to Mrs. Henderson that nobody would take her for a sailor. My purpose in knocking at the door was to ask for a glass of water. I was not wearing the polka-dot dress. I had recently drunk a carton of milk which must have splashed over my overcoat, giving it a polka-dot effect. I did not raise my overcoat to thigh level while in conversation with Mrs. Henderson.

Having been given an opportunity to reconsider that portion of my statement relating to the *Swapper's Digest*, I now believe that there may have been one or two replies to my advertisement. There may have been 1,753 replies. Certain parcels which Det.-Sgt. Cooney removed from under the floorboards in my presence may contain replies to my advertisement. I have not read any of them. I do not recognise a typewritten manuscript entitled *Kitty's Awakening*. I do not know of any invitation to attend a party in Tulse Hill for sex fun.

I am familiar with Tulse Hill. I may have been there on the evening of December 18. An important invoice had blown out of my office window on that day and I thought it might have landed in Tulse Hill. I may have been wearing a shortie nightdress under my raincoat. I often wear a shortie nightdress in the privacy of my own home as I understand there is no law against it. I wear it because it is convenient. At approximately 10 pm, on the evening of December 18, I remembered that I had not taken the dog for his usual walk. I put on a raincoat over my shortie nightdress and took him as far as the pillar box. The dog having slipped his lead and been run over by a coal-lorry I thought that rather than waste my outing I would proceed to Tulse Hill and look for the invoice.

I may have approached several householders in the Tulse Hill district with the words, 'Have you a French kitten for sale?' I was not aware that this was a password. Owing to the accident to my dog I was anxious to obtain a new pet as quickly as possible. I do not know why I asked for a French kitten. I now think that I may have asked for a *fresh* kitten, meaning one that was only a few days old.

After a conversation with my wife Noreen I now recall that I have never owned a dog. I have been taking pills for a severe migraine and these, swallowed in conjunction with beer or wine, sometimes induce a sensation of owning a dog.

I deny hailing a taxi at Tulse Hill Station at 1.43 on the morning of December 19.

Having been assured that nobody is going to get their collar felt for taking a cab, I now remember hailing a taxi at Tulse Hill Station, but deny asking the driver if he knew anything about blue movies.

The taxi took me to my home. I deny saying, 'Well, here we are at Iceberg Manor.' I deny offering the driver double fare to take me to Hampstead Heath.

Certain evidence having been shown to me, I admit to being on Hampstead Heath at 3.16 on the morning of December 19 and approaching the gentleman I now recognise as Det.-Sgt. Cooney. I regret having prevaricated about this matter, but I was of the impression that wearing false moustaches went out with Sexton Blake. I concur that if I had stuck to false moustaches instead of polka-dot dresses I would not be in the situation in which I now find myself.

I confirm that I mistook Det.-Sgt. Cooney for a sex maniac, and that I asked him for information about any lewd, filthy, degrading and obscene parties that might be going on in the vicinity. I agree that I falsely represented my wife Noreen as being available for sex fun in the event of Det.-Sgt. Cooney being able to assist me in my depraved endeavours. I now understand that my use of the words 'sizzling,' 'versatile' and 'hot pants' in respect of my wife Noreen was an offence under the Trades Description Act, and I wish to express my regret for any embarrassment, distress and disappointment caused both to my wife and Det.-Sgt. Cooney.

Take the ring and run

Marriage, you had better understand from the very beginning, is no joke. Those strip cartoons of domestic life, where the wife is always buying new hats or signalling a right-hand turn in order to dry her nail-varnish, and the husband is forever marooned in one corner of a newly-painted room, have as much to do with the real thing as your cheapskate engagement ring has to do with the Koh-i-noor diamond.

Married bliss is grim and married bliss is earnest, as you will find before you have even had time to tip the confetti out of your shoes. The problems facing two people about to live under the same roof, let alone share the same bed, are so complex and terrifying that even the kind of manual they send out in a plain wrapper prefers to gloss over them and distract the reader with unprintable euphemisms.

We will attempt to deal with some of these problems here, provided it is understood that we are merely skimming the top of the iceberg, and that Mr. and Mrs. Newlywed, sooner or later, will have to learn the hard way.

Making sucking noises

When the excitement of the honeymoon has worn off and you settle down to a lifetime of quiet evenings in front of the telly, it will slowly dawn on you that your partner is in the habit of making sucking noises, either through the medium of a hollow tooth or by introducing the tongue to the roof of the mouth.

There is nothing obscene or disgusting about this; indeed some Polynesian tribes do it all the time. But what is normal to one person may be distressing or even frightening to another. If these sucking noises are really getting on your nerves, and you are quite sure that they are not a reprisal for your own knuckle-cracking or whistling through the teeth, have a quiet word with your partner. Explain gently that if you had really wanted to spend night after night listening to a repertoire of barnyard imitations, you would have married an intelligent cocker spaniel.

Tensions in marriage

'Will I be able to satisfy her?' is supposedly the question that worries young bridegrooms most. What should worry them even more is, 'Will she be able to find the end of the Sellotape after I have finished using it?' Nothing is more infuriating than a husband or wife who, having taken solemn vows before an ordained minister to make life as cushy as possible for the party of the second part, puts the Sellotape back in the right-hand drawer of the desk without folding the end bit back to save wear and tear of the other partner's nails. It is even more infuriating when the Sellotape is put back in the *left*-hand drawer of the desk, where even a child of four ought to know it does not belong.

Preparing for bed

Ringing the changes is what keeps a marriage fresh and interesting, and nowhere is this more important than in the approach to the marriage bed. If, at precisely eleven o'clock each night for fifteen years, you have been in the habit of stretching elaborately and announcing, 'Ah, well, me for Bedfordshire,' try surprising your partner with some new or daring variation. Say, 'Ho, hum, me for beddy-byes.'

Chewing pencils

If you chew pencils, so that whenever your partner wants

to scribble a note to the milkman or to a lover, that partner is forced to handle what looks like a thin cylinder of ossified bacon-rind with a convention of death-watch beetles going on inside it, you are asking for trouble. You are asking for even more trouble if you chew ballpoint pens.

Every kind of gratification may be acceptable in marriage *provided that it is acceptable to both sides*. Chewing pencils is not. Chewing pencils is a filthy perversion. As for chewing ballpoint pens, people like you should be put away for life.

Telephone bills

In even the most deeply-satisfying partnership of minds and bodies, there may come a moment when one or other partner is arrested on suspicion of knocking the district nurse off her bicycle and interfering with her clothing. Or perhaps, God willing, the crisis may be of a more homely description: the eldest boy has been expelled for unspeakable practices behind the gymnasium (there is a separate booklet available about these), or the baby has been bitten by a poisonous spider.

Be sure, anyway, that tragedy will strike at some time or another. And at times like this, it is only natural that the wife will want to spend hours on the telephone while she acquaints her mother or closest friend with the news that this time she is leaving the swine for good. This must inevitably lead to a high telephone bill, and sardonic remarks by the husband in the order of, 'Since when has your mother been living in bloody Australia?'

Many couples solve this problem by keeping a piggy-bank next to the telephone. This item, if thrown forcibly at the wall by the husband when he discovers it to contain nothing but hairgrips, will do much to alleviate hurt pride.

Adjusting to each other

Like the mating dance of the praying mantis, marriage is a quadrille or, if you are unfamiliar with old-time dancing, a Palais Glide, in which each partner responds almost unconsciously to a pattern of preconceived movements. Thus it will quickly become established that every time you are watching television together, one partner will keep leaning forward and turning up the volume control a fraction, whereas the other partner will keep leaning forward and turning it down again.

It is best to allow these automatic and largely nervous gestures to become part of the background routine of marriage, so that eventually they are hardly noticed by either side. Open discussion on the lines of 'Wassamarrer, you get cloth ears or something?' may encourage rather than diminish the tension.

Leaving combs on the dressing table with tufts of hair sticking out of them
See our confidential leaflet, 'Leaving screwed-up tissues under the pillow in marriage.'

Father of the groom

The wedding has taken place at St. George's Church, Hanover Square, between Miss Emma Jane Fourfeathers, only daughter of Sir Douglas and Lady Fourfeathers, and Mr. Terry Spratt, eldest son of Mr. Ron Spratt, windows cleaned, no job too small or too big, our quotation no obligation, and Mrs. Spratt. After a reception held at the Ritz Hotel, the following notes fell from the lifeless fingers of Mr. Spratt as he was helped into the police van:

Lords, ladies, gentlemen, friends, Lady Fourfeathers, Sir Fourfeathers, one and all. Unaccustomed as am public speaking, feel opportunity should not go by without saying few words. Not often lady wife and self are up West; as for present erotic surroundings, never in born days. Lifetime motto however has always been speak as you find, so as find all and sundry dressed as if for Royal paddock at Ascot race-track, will try and keep speech at same exalted level. Wait for laughter.

Make mention of food and drink served, as it might be sherry, whisky, gin-and-tons, sidecars, vino, champagne, brandy with all the trimmings, chicken vollavongs, caviar on hot toast, trifle, cake, &c &c. Thank catering firm, Messrs. The Ritz. Tell one about Pakki what opens this catsmeat shop, only he has to close it again because he can't get no more cats. Wait for laughter.

Thank Sir and Lady Fourfeathers for graciously condescending to invite self and lady wife here today, also our

Terry for at long last telling us where he hid invitation, will not go into that now it will save till him and little Emma Jane get back from their honeymoon on the island of Greece. Seriously though, sincerely grateful Sir Fourfeathers for giving self and lady wife chance see how other half lives.

Sir Fourfeathers is good bloke. Proud to know him. Would like to shake him by hand. Puts self in mind of little story, stop self if heard it, about this woman with no legs and this geezer comes up and gives her one. After it is all over and he has unhooked her off of railings, she thanks him for being real gentleman —all other bleeders have left her hanging up there. Wait for laughter.

Like geezer in story, Sir Fourfeathers is gentleman in every sense of word. Is proper toff. Is definitely all right, have always thought so ever since first met him when our Terry had great misfortune to put little Emma Jane up stick. Have learned a lot more about Sir Fourfeathers since them days. Have learned to respect him. May have dirty great country house also flat in Park Lane, but grafts for living same as self. Is chairman and managing director of fourteen companies, sits on board of umpteen others, also is magistrate, so this your lucky day lads, you can tear up them parking tickets and obstruction summonses.

Now is neither time or place, but man in Sir Fourfeathers' position must often have occasion to review window cleaning contract. Country house alone must have seven hundred burnt cinders (point out this is Cockney rhyming slang for windows), not to mention numerous office blocks. Self can offer competitive quotation at favourable rates. Do not know if our Terry intends stay in family business now he has fallen on feet, but if does, place can always be found for little Emma Jane. Can always write out invoices, brew up tea, sweep floor &c &c, better than watching telly in Palace Gate while waiting for our Terry to come in off of round. As Sir Fourfeathers now one of family, will tell him what will do. All windows cleaned at 25 per cent off going rate. Cannot say fairer than that.

Thank best man for toast to bridesmaids. Point out that same include our Marlene and our Sandra. Could not help noticing big number of single men on bride's side of church today—have been told they all stockbrokers, big advertising men, company directors, you name it. While our Marlene nothing write home about as regards looks, has got good head on shoulders and has been to secretarial school so could write up books, make out swindle sheets &c &c, in short would be asset. Is good plain cook. Squint could be put right if necessary funds forthcoming. As for our Sandra, is supposed to be engaged to mate of our Terry's but this can always be got out of. As self has always told her, marry a bleeding barrow boy and you won't go no further in life, you have got to look after number one, why not wait for Mr. Right and have own big house, big car &c &c. So our Marlene and our Sandra both definitely available, get in there lads what are you waiting for.

Tell one about this bloke who goes to doctor and says doctor doctor, am getting married and do not know how to go about it. Doctor says, just put hand on her belly and say I love you. So, bloke gets married, goes on honeymoon, puts hand on bird's belly and says I love you. Bird says, lower, So bloke says (put on low voice), I love you. Wait for laughter.

This brings self to subject of our Terry and little Emma Jane. Not losing son, gaining daughter is way self looks at it. May all troubles be little ones. Wish them all would wish selves, if as happy as self and self's old dutch, cannot go far wrong. Will not presume offer them no advice, they could teach self also Sir and Lady Fourfeathers thing or two if you was to ask self. All will say is, hope bedsprings at Ritz Hotel also on island of Greece is in better nick than them at No. 4 Peterloo Buildings, talk about creak creak creak, self is only surprised they never had bleeding ceiling down. If got time, tell one about dog chucking bucket of water over this honeymoon couple. Wait for laughter. Ask Lady Fourfeathers if she gets it. If she says no, say why not, don't tell self Sir Fourfeathers is past it.

Last but not least, would like to scotch rumour that our Terry was after little Emma Jane for what could get. May have put her in pod, has never denied it, but was not first pig in trough by long chalk. Could mention certain guards officer, no names no pack drill, also certain young geezer here today, cannot pick him out, all look same in evening dress, like bleeding penguins. Also not true he went sniffing round her for her money. Did not know she had all that much, thought at first she was high-class Mayfair tart. Anyway, why she hanging about in Hackney boozer if not looking for rough trade, she wanted him now she has got him.

Still, all that water under bridge. Would once again thank Sir Moneybags, beg his pardon, Sir Fourfeathers, for sit-down nosh-up, would ask all present to be upstanding, if so capable at this stage—wait for laughter—and drink second toast to our Terry and little Emma Jane, this time coupled with name of little stranger. Wait for applause. Tell one about Jewish doctor and bloke with no nose. Do imitation of blind man drinking cup of tea. Pick up wedding cake and ask Lady Fourfeathers if she would like a bit. If she says yes, say why, is Sir Fourfeathers keeping you short of it?

Ideal summer girl

It's not given to all of us to be H. E. Bates, so there is no point in starting anything about the yellow strings of laburnum flower that we are unable to finish.

Beyond doubt it was summer. Certain unidentified birds sang in a variety of trees. The flowers, whether laburnum or otherwise, flourished.

The scene was a patch of arable land which may or may not have been a meadow.

To paraphrase Peter de Vries she was stark naked except for a PVC raincoat, dress, net stockings, undergarments, shoes, rain-hat, gloves, umbrella and a bucket-bag containing Kleenex tissues. She wandered along the hedge-row gathering the white hedge-flowers, or hedge-blossom, from the—well, hedge-trees. If she had concentrated more on the sheets of buttercups that dazzled under a high blue sky we would have been on botanically safer ground, but I approached her just the same.

I asked her name and she said it: 'Rose.' What else, in weather like this?

I explained that on this ideal cuckoo day I was looking for a girl on whom I would eventually be able to look back through the mists of time and remember as the lost ideal of that high distant summer. She asked me what high distant summer and I replied this one: the present one. The bluebells were going out all over Europe and they would not bloom again, if blooming was what they had been doing, in our lifetime. I wanted to remember the last English rose of that last high carefree June before the world grew dark.

She asked me why the world would have grown dark and I said there were any number of reasons why it would have grown dark. A world holocaust, for example, or a slump, or the nationalisation of land. The point was, if she would just listen and stop interrupting, to be able to look back on a carefree bloody June with a carefree golden girl. We would make daisy-chains, wander by the river tickling trout and other fish. There would be sticklebacks, king-fishers, hawthorn, willow-herb, reeds of various kinds, cow-slips. We might not be able to classify such flora and fauna but this I could promise her: sheets of buttercups dazzling under a high blue sky. Any silly fool could recognise butter-cups. We would lie down in them and our hands would touch in the red evening twilight.

She raised a point about the colour scheme. Was the sky high blue or red evening?

I said that it would have been high blue to begin with but it would have become red evening later. If we stayed around long enough it would become golden night, and we would lie on our sheets of buttercups listening to the whip-poor-will.

She said that she had not understood much of what I was talking about but she thought she had caught the general drift. For her own part she was a Danish au pair girl called Jorgenson. Her employer, a Mr. Rogers who was in the motor accessories business, called her Rose because he could not pronounce her first name.

She lived in the Big House across the meadow. (Actually, when we face facts, it was not so much a meadow as the site for six bungalows. The full dark song of the blackbird, or it might have been a thrush or an escaped parrot, was lost in the low throbbing of a cement-mixing machine.)

It was an ideal magpie day and we walked together over the sheets of buttercups and the hot tarpaulins towards the Big House. When I say Big House, I suppose more accur-ately it was a Span maisonette. But the garden was heavy

with blue hibiscus—blue hibiscus? Blue something, anyway. Not daffodils. Irises, possibly—and the air was still,
and it was an ideal chaffinch day.

'You will come to my room?' she said, but I had not
planned on that at all. I asked her, what about the sheets
of buttercups?

'It will be damp,' she said, and indeed the high blue
sky had turned an ominous grey as if the shadow of a world
holocaust or a slump was already falling across that last
golden June. I imagined her room with its open window
overlooking the thick current bushes; it would be heavy
with the scent of—well, currants, I suppose. There would
be blue hibiscus or irises in cool stone jars, and tree ferns
pressed in the pages of *What's On in London*. There would
be good rough cider from the wood, or Scotch and ginger ale
for those who preferred it.

So I agreed that we would go to her room.

'But not today,' she said. 'We have only just met.'

I pointed out that this was the whole charm of the deal:
you meet this total stranger in a meadow on this golden day
before the world has grown dark; the pair of you make
beasts of yourselves on sheets of buttercups under a high
blue, or ominous grey, sky; and then you stroll off inde-
pendently, never to meet again. The thing was practically
folklore.

She said: 'Today I must go to the launderette, and then
bring the children from the ice-skating rink. We will meet
again. I would like to see *Dr. Zhivago*.'

We arranged to meet when the hawthorn would be in
bud and the lush grass covered in cuckoo spit (we would
take a groundsheet) and the martin would be singing its
plaintive/jolly song.

This left it all a bit vague. I went back to the meadow a
couple of times between June and October. There was a
bird singing, but it sounded more like a seagull to me. The
flowers were gone. The bungalows were built. I never saw
her again but I remembered, such as it was, that ideal
buttercup day.

One of our spies is Miss Inge

Half a million civil servants have been warned to watch
out for a new security risk. Beware the au pair girl from
a Communist country, they are told in memorandum. She
could be a potential spy in your home

—*Daily Mail*

Mr. Whitsun Bank-Holiday, for the Prosecution, said that
this was a shocking case. It was a case of a so-called au pair
girl—the accused, Olga Karamazova—coming to these
shores, inveigling herself into the employ of a decent English household, and repaying their hospitality by embark-
ing on a career of espionage.

Mr. Whitsun Bank-Holiday said that he would be as
brief as possible. Mr. T. Drinker was a senior civil servant
at the Ministry of Defence, with special responsibility towards the survival of the Queen's subjects in the event of a
nuclear attack. Mrs. Drinker was a keen gardener and a
member of the Wimbledon Cheery Folks, an amateur concert party. There were two children of the marriage—
Kevin and Barbara, aged five and seven respectively.

The court would hear that until November 1970 the
Drinker family's au pair was one Netochka Nezvanova, from
Portugal. Senorita Nezvanova had been diligent in her
work and indeed satisfactory in every way. She was a keen
'ham' radio enthusiast and often allowed the children to
play with her Morse tapper. It was only when some men
came to fetch her in a big black car that her period of

employment was reluctantly terminated.

What more natural than that the Drinker family should go to the Vladimir Lenin Domestic Agency and Institute of Cultural Research, the same agency which had supplied Senorita Nezvanova, to find a replacement.

It was no part of the prosecution's task to question the integrity of the Vladimir Lenin Domestic Agency. It was a reputable firm which had occupied the same registered offices—the second bench along as you went round Kensington Pond in a clockwise direction—since 1958. Having shown Mr. Drinker a microfilm copy of Olga Karamazova's references in good faith the Agency's obligations were discharged. Mr. Drinker duly deposited the Agency's fee in a hollow oak tree near the Albert Memorial, and the accused subsequently left her home in Switzerland and joined the Drinker household later that same week.

Mrs. Drinker would tell the court that Olga Karamazova appeared to settle down happily enough in the Wimbledon menage, and that every effort was made to accommodate her. A keen amateur photographer and homing-pigeon enthusiast, she was readily given permission to convert the cupboard under the stairs into a darkroom, and the attic into a pigeon loft. She was interested in the radio equipment that Senorita Nezvanova had left behind, and was allowed to borrow it. Having joined a social club—the Central Committee for Au Pair Girls in Exile—she was rarely denied an afternoon off to attend its meetings. She was, despite her eccentric habit of eating slips of paper with writing on them, encouraged to take her meals with the family.

It would be for the jury to decide whether, in view of subsequent events, Olga Karamazova might be said to have bitten the hand that fed her. Whether she arrived at the Drinker establishment from Switzerland with the deliberate, preconceived intention of spying, or whether she later succumbed to temptation, was neither here nor there.

Mrs. Drinker would swear on oath that in June of this year the affairs of the Cheery Folks concert party bore

heavily on her mind. She had undertaken to write, produce and appear in a sketch tentatively entitled, 'At the
Dentist's.' During this same month Mr. Drinker was greatly
occupied with a master-plan of all the deep air raid shelters
in Britain which he was preparing for his masters at the
Ministry of Defence. Mr. Drinker was obliged to bring
work home at weekends. Mrs. Drinker had her gardening
activities as well as the Cheery Folks. It fell to Olga Karamazova, during this hectic period, to take sole charge of
the children, Kevin and Barbara.

Both the Drinkers would agree in evidence that at first
they had no grounds for complaint. Karamazova, like any
Swiss girl new to London, was interested in the tourist
attractions of the city, and she seemed eager and willing
to take the children on a series of outings to such places
as London Docks, Trafalgar Square, RAF Station Uxbridge, the basement of the War Office and so on and so
forth.

However, the jury would learn from Mr. Drinker that
at about this time Olga Karamazova began to take an
interest in his briefcase. She was always present in the
morning to hand it to him as he left for the Ministry; always
there in the evening to relieve him of it when he arrived
home. On several occasions, according to Mr. Drinker,
she said that the briefcase was in a shabby condition and
offered to take it down to her darkroom to give it a good
polish. It would be for the jury to decide whether the
accused took an unusual interest in Mr. Drinker's briefcase.

Mr. Whitsun Bank-Holiday said that on the fourth of
July, Olga Karamazova had charge of the children for the
entire day. Barbara and Kevin were too young to appear in
the witness box, but they had made depositions, and in those
sworn depositions they had said, in part, as follows: 'Nana
came to our room at approximately 8.23 am. She said to us,
"And zees morning, we go to zee secret missile base, no?
Barbara will carry zee binoculars, Kevin zee camera, and I
zee sandwiches." We agreed to this plan.'

Witness after witness would prove that Olga Karamazova took the children nowhere near the secret missile base that day. She led them, instead, to the Ministry of Defence, on the thin pretext that, having forgotten a dolly belonging to the child Barbara, she would have to borrow Mr. Drinker's key and return to Wimbledon.

The commissionaire would say that Karamazova arrived during Mr. Drinker's lunch-hour. That she knew full well it was Mr. Drinker's lunch-hour would be proved in due course. She was escorted to Mr. Drinker's office where his briefcase lay on the desk. That Karamazova seized the briefcase and then hurried the children down the fire-escape would also be proved to the hilt.

Karamazova, the jury would hear, was arrested in Green Park shortly after she had handed the briefcase to a Swiss compatriot named Ivan Dostoievsky. Dostoievsky, unfortunately, had been able to make his escape to Zurich, with the briefcase.

Mr. Whitsun Bank-Holiday, in conclusion, said that no doubt the jury would be curious to know what the briefcase contained. It contained, as the accused must have well known, a complete draft of the sketch, 'At the Dentist's' which Mrs. Drinker had written for the Cheery Folks concert party, and which Mr. Drinker habitually carried with him in order to study the leading role, that of Dr. I. Pullem.

Thanks to Olga Karamazova's duplicity, thanks to her ingratitude, thanks to her treachery, that sketch was now in the hands of a foreign power. No doubt it was only a matter of time before a pirated version of it appeared on Swiss television. As for British concert parties—an institution which every decent Englishman held dear—their activities had been set back by at least twelve months. It was a grave charge upon which Olga Karamazova stood indicted and one which, if the jury agreed that the case was proved, deserved to be visited with the full rigour of the law.

Blowing up suburbia

'But why us?' bleat the plaintive owners of 'Enidsholme' and 'Agnesdene,' Pear Tree Close, off Dairymead Avenue, Orchard Farm Estate, Birmingham.

A difficult question to answer, gentlemen. Why not 'Erzanmine' and 'Dunroamin,' Ullswater Crescent, off Windermere Road, Lakeview Estate, Liverpool? Or 'Joyceandbill' and 'Kosikot' of Turner Approach, off Constable Drive, Tate Gallery Estate, Dagenham? Why not, come to think of it, the whole of Dagenham? Why not the razor blade factories on the Great West Road, the Chiswick flyover, Harlow New Town, the caravan parks of Lytham St. Annes, the M1 and all who sail on it, most of the South Bank, the entire city of Glasgow and its environs, all Wimpy bars, nearly all shoe-shops, every office building erected since 1946 with the omission of Centrepoint, all municipal housing estates without exception, all petrol stations and the boroughs of Wembley, Ruislip, Hounslow, Uxbridge, Croydon and Tottenham, to name but a few?

Come, friendly bombs, and fall on Slough, wrote the bard of bad taste. Unfortunately we have not bombs enough for a catchment area of that magnitude—not even enough for one little cul-de-sac of semis, nestling between the bottling plant and the bowling alley, and sheltered anyway from direct attack by the elevated road to Wales which looms over 'Redroofs' and 'Inglenook' and 'Elmsview' like a gigantic spare-room ceiling. All we have is one small keg of gunpowder—just enough to blow 'Enidsholme' and 'Agnesdene' off the face of the earth. No more than a token reprisal—we can start the thousand bomber raids later, when the appeal fund's been properly launched.

The aim, quite simply, is to make it possible to travel the length and breadth of England without the gnawing suspicion, which presently occurs, that one is doing no more than to drive round and round the South Circular Road. Clearly, since we have to start somewhere, the first thing to go must be that double-fronted monument to all that is ghastly in this sceptr'd isle, the semi-detached villa.

I pick 'Enidsholme' rather than 'Dunroamin' or 'Kosikot' because while 'Dunroamin' has a stone toadstool in its front garden and 'Kosikot' has a hall window the shape of a porthole, through which can be clearly seen a plaster effigy of a goose in flight, 'Endisholme' boasts a plastic sun-dial, which is under strong suspicion of having been given away with a suite of eeziplan uncut-moquette lounge furniture. This plastic sun-dial, to compound the offence, has not been decently laid to rest in the Jiffifix garden shed with the now unfashionable Chianti-bottle table-lamps, nor has it been set on fire; rather has it been given a place of honour in the centre of a diamond-shaped plot of grass that has a border of half-bricks round it. Furthermore, the title or legend 'Enidsholme' has been inscribed in gothic letters on a cross section of polished beechwood that hangs by two lengths of chromium chain below the porch, unlike the titles or legends 'Dunroamin' and 'Kosikot' which have only been painted on their respective gates, although admittedly one of those gates is in the shape of a ship's wheel.

Turning now to 'Enidsholme's' neighbour 'Agnesdene,' that undesirable residence draws the short straw for no other reason that whither 'Enidsholme' goeth, 'Agnesdene' goeth also—in this case sky-high. They were conceived and brought forth together, mirror-images of one another on an architect's drawing-board, or more likely on an accountant's costing-sheet. Each is the other's doppelgänger: neither can exist without the existence of the other

—but which is the shadow? Their rooms are identical, except that the fawn-tiled fireplaces with the green lozenges are at opposite ends; in the spring-cleaning season the open windows of 'Enidsholme' reflect the open windows of 'Agnesdene' which reflect the open windows of 'Enidsholme', identical pictures diminishing into infinity like a painting by Magritte. Their fortunes are bound together: if 'Enidsholme' increases in value by ten per cent, so does 'Agnesdene'; if 'Agnesdene's' drains are blocked the effluent rises in 'Enidsholme's' sink-unit. Their owners are more than neighbours, they are voluntary Siamese twins, joined forever by the tissue of the party wall.

And so 'Enidsholme' and 'Agnesdene' will go together when they go. This, I hope, will be in the merry month of August, when the owners of 'Enidsholme' are playing bingo in a holiday camp in Majorca and the owners of 'Agnesdene' are watching ITV in the Crow's Nest Bar of a motel in Cornwall. I do realise that 'Please to remember the twenty-first of August, gunpowder, treason and plot' doesn't scan as well as the original, but the last thing we want is to be strapped in a tubular garden chair while 'Enidsholme' extracts the confession and 'Agnesdene' makes us all a nice cup of instant coffee. So bear with me through the long hot summer; don't clench your teeth when 'Enidsholme' commences to fashion his privet hedge in the shape of castle battlements; don't flinch when 'Agnesdene' adopts a family of stone garden pixies, one of them holding a fishing-rod. The end is nigh.

The first item on the agenda is to get an accurate ground-plan of both sets of premises. Since we are working to a tight budget we will save ourselves an unnecessary journey to Birmingham by proceeding instead to Ruislip, where, posing as encyclopedia salesmen, we will gain access to all that dwelling-house situate and known as 'Fairlawns,' Shelley Way, off Keats Road South, Patience Strong Estate. A moment's glance will tell us that except for minor details such as a dinette hatch here and a Slimmex radiator unit there, 'Fairlawns' and 'Enidsholme' are identical in all respects (as indeed are 'Fairlawns' and 'Agnesdene,' except of course that 'Agnesdene' would be the other way round). So, while the lady of the house is examining our specimen copy of volume one in the simulated Skivertex binding she will love to handle, we whip out our cameras and take photographs of her sun-trap lounge. We then wish her a civil good morning (if we can sell her a set of encyclopedias before we leave, so much the better; kegs of gunpowder do not come cheap) and hurry home to develop our film. What we then have is a faithful blueprint of the inside of 'Enidsholme.' Reverse the negative and we will have a faithful blueprint of the inside of 'Agnesdene.'

Having decided under which leatherette pouffe or laminated plastic telly-trolley we propose to deposit our explosive, we now proceed to Pear Tree Close, off Dairymead Avenue, Orchard Farm Estate, Birmingham. There remains the problem of access. It is very likely that 'Enidsholme' has left a key inside the letter-box on the end of a piece of string, the easier for one of the neighbours to get in and feed the tropical fish. 'Agnesdene,' possibly, has hidden a latchkey under the doormat for the benefit of a married daughter from Solihull who will be coming in to air the beds. Failing either of these contingencies, we must resume our pose as encyclopedia salesmen and kick the door in.

We divide our gunpowder into equal portions and deposit one half in 'Enidsholme' and the other in 'Agnesdene.' We synchronise our watches. We light the blue touch-paper and retire. Within seconds we are rewarded for our industry by a wondrous sight—the timid hopes of the building societies blown sky-high, the future of gimcrack architecture lost in a giant catherine-wheel of bay-windows and portholes and flying pebbledash, the Englishman's cautious dream of half a mini-castle over. Up and up soars that monstrous doll's house, its rateable value depreciating by five per cent every second; soon it splits in two in a burst of sparks, and the burned-out shells of 'Enidsholme' and 'Agnesdene' soar on the wind like paper silhouettes.

On the stippled walls of semis all over England there is a shudder, and then a monstrous flight of plaster geese takes wing, dips over the dormitory suburbs and disappears into the clouds in perfect V-formation.

Letters tied with blue

Mr. Charles Dickens presents his compliments to Mr. Currer Bell and regrets that he is no longer the Editor of *Bentley's Miscellany*.

Mr. Dickens is unused to receiving *a whole packing case* full of unsolicited MSS in an illegible hand, and is so closely occupied with his own work that he cannot possibly read it.

Mr. Dickens suggests that Mr. Bell might submit his work to the *Leeds Intelligencer*. He would diffidently put forward the suggestion that, were Mr. Bell to pay the postage himself, rather than dispatching the packing case COD, Mr. Bell's chances of at least a part of his work achieving publication might be enhanced.

Dear Sir,

You will have thought me strangely tardy in acknowledging your letter; the fact is that Mr. Currer Bell is not known in this district, and it is only by the fortuitous circumstances that my brother Branwell works in a temporary capacity as the Haworth postman (it is his intention to become Editor of *Blackwood*), that your generous epistle reached me. It was in a pair of breeches left by my brother on Dewsbury Moor last evening.

Be assured I shall do what I can to profit by your wise and good counsel. You have been so unsparing and frank in your advice that I feel emboldened to be frank also, and to confess that I am no more 'Mr. Currer Bell' than I am the Man in the Moon. I am at present one of three sisters all of whom are of delicate constitution; I say 'at present' for only God in his mercy knows whether there will still be three of us when this letter reaches you. As I write I hear my poor sister Anne coughing; she bears it without complaint but I wonder whether she will last the night. Yet a word from you, were you to trouble yourself to read some of her own effusions, would ameliorate her sufferings. We have taken to heart your strictures about illegibility, and if our health be spared and time vouchsafed to us, we mean to copy out our entire works in a fair hand and dispatch them to you for the value of an opinion.

> *I am, Sir, yours truly,*
> C. Brontë

Dear Madam,

Pray do *not* put yourself to the trouble & expense of dispatching your sister's manuscripts, or your own manuscripts, or anybody's manuscripts, to me. The Printer is waiting for 12pp of *Nickleby* and a double number of *Oliver,* and in any case I am obliged to go to Ramsgate tomorrow. If your brother has connexions with *Blackwood* I would venture the opinion, that your work would be better lodged there than with

> *Your obdt. servant,*
> Charles Dickens

PS. I trust your sister's cough is better.

Dear Sir,

I fear that you will burn my letter upon perusing the signature but if you will read it through, you will perhaps rather pity than spurn the distress of mind which could prompt my communication.

It would be *useless* to approach *Blackwood,* who have commenced a spiteful vendetta against my brother, and who threaten legal proceedings should he attempt to communicate with them again in any way. While awaiting the reply to an application for the Editorship of the *Edinburgh Review*, my brother has gained employment as a porter at the Sowerby Bridge Railway Station, and it was in this capacity that he dispatched the crate of manuscripts to you, the day before your kind letter admonishing us not to do so was received. Now that the deed is done, dare I hope that you will not turn us away without a crumb from your table? You have advised us, encouraged us; now we hold on to your interest as we would to life. You have generously inquired about my sister's health: she is mercifully still with us, but now my sister Emily has sickened, and a more pallid countenance I have yet to behold. The winter is hard and cold; the moors are a wilderness, featureless, solitary, saddening. We live only for a word from *you*. *You* have shown that interest, that it is to *you* we turn in the anguish of these dark moments.

Yours respectfully,
C. Brontë

PS. My brother begs me to inquire whether a new Editor of *Bentley's Miscellany* has yet been appointed.

Dear Mr. Dickens,

Six months of silence since we dispatched our manuscripts to you! Only the cry of the curlew, the wind on the heath and the solicitor's letter forbidding my brother Branwell from writing to you again, to ease our solitude!

Did the crate of MSS perhaps not reach you? No matter; it is God's will. The hard frost and the keen wind have done nothing for my sisters' constitution; but if they are spared, they shall each write at least one more novel before they are called to eternity. My sister Emily begs me to inquire, what your opinion is of the title 'Withering Heights.'

Forgive me, Master, if I adopt the course of writing to you again. Day and night I find neither rest nor peace. If I sleep I am disturbed by tormenting dreams in which I see *you*. How can I endure life if I make no effort to ease its sufferings? You showed me a *little* interest, when you advised me to write to the *Leeds Intelligencer*, now I need the continuance of that interest as I need bread. The winter has been bitterly cold; life at Haworth wears away; one day resembles another. I hope, I pine, for a letter from you; day follows day and no letter comes, unless a missive from you was among the batch my brother sold to a bookseller in Bradford, to pay for medicine.

Perhaps you received our manuscripts but cannot read our handwriting. As soon as I shall have saved enough money to go to London I shall go there, and visit you, and read you our works from the beginning to the end. If you have compassion, you will not turn me away. I need very little affection from those I love.

> *Yours respectfully,*
> Charlotte Brontë

Dear Miss Brontë,

I am correcting the proofs of *Master Humphrey's Clock*, *The Old Curiosity Shop* and *Barnaby Rudge* and have but a minute to spare, as the Printer's Devil is at my elbow.

It pains me, I assure you with real sincerity, to be obliged to say that *neither Mrs. Dickens* nor I can see you, should you come to London, nor can I read your papers, nor can I assist your brother to secure employment on *Bentley's Miscellany*.

I know it may be unpalatable to you that I should do so, but I cannot forbear writing to you—I know it is an impertinence—that I am strongly of the opinion that you should turn from the contemplation of the melancholic aspects of your life, induced no doubt by the long Yorkshire winter, to bright hopes of the happiness which I am sure must be in store for you and your sisters.

I am taking the liberty of inclosing a copy of *Pickwick Papers*; it may 'cheer you up.'

> *Your obdt. servant,*
> Charles Dickens

Dear Mr. Dickens,

I must thank you first for the autographed edition of *Pickwick*, which I confess I did not read, but which remained under my pillow until this morning, when my brother inadvertently auctioned it at the local inn.

With great reluctance, I must turn to the more painful portion of your letter. The reference to Mrs. Dickens, with its heavy underscoring, has not escaped me. You know that I love you; I tell you frankly that I have tried to forget you: I have sought other occupations; I have even written to Mr. Thackeray; but *you* saw my heart's woe, *you* discovered my soul's anguish. I did not think of marriage. Reason tells me that I shall never marry; my life is what I expected it to be, a life of solitude, remembrance, longing. But I am not made of stone. If a woman should be ashamed of feeling love, then there is nothing noble, faithful, truthful in this earth. The cold northern spring is upon us once more; my poor sisters are worn out; my unhappy brother has been dismissed for intemperance; my youth goes like a dream. My box is packed; I will go anywhere that you direct me; I will ask for nothing that you do not wish to give. Do not deny me the sweet delight of seeing you but once, for that would be to tear from me my only prospect of joy on earth.

> *Yours respectfully,*
> Charlotte Brontë

Dear Miss Brontë,

The missus is out, and I write in haste.

If you are disposed for an adventure, I take horse next Sunday at 10 for York. I know a good 'ouse there, the Blue Lion, where we can have a red hot chop, and oyster puddings, and weal patties, and mulled wine. And then what larks! what tumbles! what prospect of joy on earth! what heaven!

I shall sign the 'visitors' book' in the name of C. Bell

and tell them I am expecting my Spouse from visiting her sick sisters at Haworth.

Faithfully Yours,
C. D.

Dear Sir,

My sister Charlotte has requested me to write and say that she will be unable to attend the literary soiree at York, as she has developed a cough.

Now sir, *read what I write.*

I shall attend upon you in York. Attend to me in return and act upon what I say! I may appear to write with conceited assurance *but I do not*; I believe in my own originality, and on that ground I desire from you that you should read, and read in front of me, specimens of my writing which I shall bring from Haworth, and then tell me openly whether I do not stand head and shoulders above wretched hacks such as yourself.

I shall be staying at the Blue Lion and shall expect you. CONDEMN NOT UNHEARD! If you wish for a professional rival God grant you may get one in

Patrick Branwell Brontë

Mr. Charles Dickens presents his compliments to Mr. Patrick Branwell Brontë, and regrets that his visit to York has been cancelled, as he is leaving immediately for America.

Gone fishing

As Hon. Secy of the Clogthorpe Angling Socy (affiliated) I have been asked by Herbert to furnish the committee with a verbatim explanation of how the socy came to get unfavourable write-up in chap xi of the library book *Clogthorpe: The Problem of Leisure in an Urban Community* by Geo. Sneap.

First and foremost, let me say straight off that in my personal opinion we came out of it better than the Cemetery Street pitch and toss school, chap viii refers, also that even if Geo. Sneap makes us out to be a bunch of silly b———s, he does not tar us with the same brush as he classes the bellringers, who he implies in so many words that they want their heads tested. See Appendix F: *A culture in decline*.

Geo. Sneap accompanied us in an observatory capacity to the Pride of Yorkshire Silver Shield chub contest (best weight) at Knaresborough on August Bank Holiday Saturday last. How Geo. Sneap came to be chucked into the River Nidd has already been explained in the so-called press report, THREW SOCIOLOGIST IN RIVER ALLEGATION, attached cutting from *Clogthorpe Mercury* refers. My brief is to satisfy the committee how Geo. Sneap came to describe angling as a dying sport when one-nought-seven (107) members and affiliated members definitely set off.

First and foremost, embussing. I spoke to Herbert

verbally three times—once on the bowling green, once over a game of fives-and-threes at the Paternosters Arms, and once in the gents' urinal of the Buff's Lodge— and definitely made representations to him that we should not embus outside the Corn Exchange on the same day as they were holding the Cage Birds Show on above premises. Herbert promised to expedite this explosive situation but did not. Result: we are all sitting in the coach, waiting for L. Hetherington (capt) to finish exercising his whippet, when suddenly Thos Longhurst (social secy) asks Geo. Sneap if he has ever seen a black canary. Upon Geo. Sneap opining that he has not, and some of the lads laying bets that it has been dyed, twenty-eight (28) members and affiliated members troop out of the coach and into the Cage Birds Show. We waited half an hour, and only Thos Longhurst (social secy), Geo. Sneap and B. Liversedge (president-elect) returned to the coach, the other lads having joined a queue for cheap budgie seed. See favourable write-up on pets in chap iv.

B. Refreshment stop. First and foremost we should never have stopped at the Terminus Inn, because you as a committee know full well what L. Hetherington (capt) is like when he has got a few inside him. We should have stopped at the Miners' Rest where L. Hetherington (capt) is barred for hitting that woman and would have had to wait in the coach. (Cutting glued in minute book, STRUCK WOMAN WHO TROD ON WHIPPET STORY, refers.) However, this was not implemented and we stopped at the Terminus. Result: I as hon secy am sitting in the snug with Geo. Sneap, trying to get a free mention in his book of Herbert's trout ($5\frac{3}{4}$ lb, caught on R. Wharfe, 5/4/67) when in comes L. Hetherington (capt) and bets some of the lads that they cannot race to the top of Terminus Street and back before the pub clock has finished striking twelve. Eighteen (18) members and affiliated members took L. Hetherington (capt) up on his bet, and out of these, thirteen (13) plus three bystanders including B. Liversedge (president-elect) were arrested in the argument that followed. Attached cutting, ANGLERS BROKE GLASS IN PUB FRACAS JPS TOLD, refers.

So far, so good. We still had sixty-five (65) members and affiliated members (not bad compared to fiasco on Blackwater Reservoir last Easter—see Appendix A of library book: *Drinking Patterns: A Tentative Analysis*. Blame this on blabmouth Thos Longhurst (social secy), one sniff of barmaid's apron and everything comes out). Of these stalwart members, forty-three (43) definitely clocked in at the River Nidd, not two (2) as stated by Geo. Sneap, *Clogthorpe: The Problem of Leisure in an Urban Community*, p. 142. First and foremost, why as a so-called sociologist didn't he bother to go round the back of the Nidd Arms, where he would have seen eighteen (18) of the lads getting up a cock-fight, also private room of Fisherman's Rest (usual wrestling—six of the lads accounted for). This I admit leaves a discrepancy of thirty-nine (39) lads between what left the Terminus Inn; p. 189 of Geo. Sneap's library book refers:

'One of the few genuinely working class interests not corroded by television and the bingo hall is the game of nipsy, a primitive kind of golf played with a wooden peg instead of a ball. As many as fifty miners might take part in a nipsy school—possibly because of the opportunities it presents for heavy gambling.'

Geo. Sneap does not give credit where it is due, because thirty-nine (39) out of that nipsy school were definitely members of the Clogthorpe Angling Socy (affiliated). They joined in above school when we had to debus at the York Road toilet facilities at Herbert's request. We always expect to lose a few lads to the nipsy school, but this was an unusually high number due to the presence at said event of a team from *World in Action*. Attached cutting, BROKE TV CAMERA IN SCUFFLE SAY POLICE, refers.

3. Choice of judge for fishing match. I have made representations to Herbert on several occasions, both in the urinal of the Buff's Lodge and in a private capacity, to the effect that D. Patterson (judge) does not know a chub

from a tin of salmon. As Hubert has personally crossed swords with D. Patterson (judge) in re that disputed bream on Shoddy Mill Ponds last summer (see cutting framed in darts room: BEST FRIEND TRIED TO DROWN ME CLAIMS ANGLER), he cannot blame me for words being exchanged on River Nidd and spoiling a good day's fishing. I definitely did not shove Geo. Sneap in R. Nidd, as wrongly stated in Clogthorpe Magistrates' Court. I shoved D. Patterson (judge) in R. Nidd. D. Patterson (judge) grabbed hold of Herbert, Herbert grabbed hold of me in my capacity as hon secy, and I grabbed hold of Geo. Sneap. I definitely did apologise and pointed out it was his own fault for sticking his nose in and should get back to London with the other pansy-boys.

In conclusion, please excuse pencil as am using the filler of my fountain pen as float for glass-fibre fixed-reel rod. Am getting good results with this and suggest suitable write-up in *Angling Times* to counterbalance unfavourable publicity from Geo. Sneap.

The truth shall make you free!

The Kosycot Happiness Through Effort, Solidarity And Never Owing Nobody For Nothing Always Paid Cash On The Nail It Has Been Our One Rule In Life family collective voluntarily and unanimously gave up its Sunday lie-in recently in order to hold a spontaneous meeting for the purposes of self-criticism and to demonstrate solidarity against the running dogs of imperialism at No. 43 next door what has the radio blaring out at all hours, as for their son Barry he is nothink but a jackal of the reactionary capitalist system and a cheeky young devil, why don't they make him get his hair cut.

Present at this voluntary assembly were Our Dad, Our Mum, Our Gran, Our Noreen, Our Noreen's husband Barry, Young Kevin, and Mr. Nightingale what was present in an honorary capacity being as how him and Our Dad always have a couple of pints at The Crooked Billet of a Sunday dinner-time, it is invariably the Crooked Billet these days, have given up The Green Man completely, landlord does not properly understand the nature of the class struggle also beer is like dishwater.

Our Dad rose at 10.30 a.m. and received a standing ovation. The family collective passed a unanimous and spontaneous resolution that Young Kevin should give over chucking bits of toast.

Our Dad said that he had only this to say, everythink was blooming marvellous, in fact it was all a very good thing, what the State had done for the common man. Under the corrupt filthy swinish Tory capitalist system, mark you he was going back a bit now, he (Our Dad) had been nothink but a lousy stinking bus conductor, twenty-two quid a week, overtime if you was lucky, whereas since the elimination of economic exploitation and what with Old Jack retiring through his leg, he had now risen to be an Inspector on the Astounding Joy Through Satisfaction Public Transport Facility, what used to be the old London Transport.

He was earning good money and was pleased to report that by applying true revolutionary principles and cutting down on fags, the family collective had now reached its target of sixty-four quid for new telly, Mr. Nightingale knew where he could get colour set for that price, ask no questions get no lies told. The clothing club norm had also been reached so no problem about school blazer for Young Kevin, as for holiday at the Mao Tse-Tung Hotel on the Costa Brava it was definitely fixed, so don't nobody start changing their minds and wanting to go to the Spirit of the People caravan site at Southend, forty quid for the week and take your own bleeding food, we (the family collective) should cocoa.

However, Our Dad was forced to pass the remark that while the family collective was keeping up to scratch as regards building for socialism through diligence and frugality, somebody was still putting toffee papers down the lav. He did not blame Our Gran: the silly old twat was a victim of the political oppression of the peasants back in the old days and could no more grasp the Marxist philosophy of dialectical materialism than pigs could fly.

All Our Dad was asking for was just that bit of give and take. If the family collective played fair by him, he would play fair by the family collective. If, on the other hand, the family collective wanted to do things the hard way, there was always the Wellbeing Of The Masses Old People's Home for them what refused to toe the line, same as Our Noreen's husband Barry, if he had been told not to lean his bicycle against the sideboard once he had been told a million times, it was about time him and Noreen got a flat of their own. Long live the People's Revolution.

Our Mam, in proposing a toast to the Leader of the People's Democracy without whose inspiration the struggle of the masses would have been in vain, said that Our Dad was a paper tiger. He was always wittering. Nobody was perfect and she herself had made errors and in future would strive to correct her mistaken ideas. Give you an example: contrary to the teachings of the Strength Through Nourishment Cut Out And Keep Recipe Page in the People's Daily, Our Mam had been over-whisking her egg whites, result being that the cheese soufflé had been coming out all runny. By applying the three main rules of socialist discipline, she would see that this did not happen again.

However, Our Dad should take a look in the mirror and correct his own tendency towards negativism before going on about other people's toffee papers and bicycles. If he had built a bike shed back in the corrupt era of two thousand years of feudalism, same as what he always said he was going to do, he would have no need to be moaning on about scratches on the sideboard during the present enlightened dawning of a true communist system.

Also, it was all very well putting money on one side for colour tellies what had fallen of the back of a lorry, but Our Mam could not manage on the housekeeping. Due to the fact that consumer goods were no longer monopolised by a privileged class but were available to the masses, prices had gone up somethink shocking. Also, if the wife of the enemy of progress and toady of the bourgeoisie at No. 43 could have three new coats a year, there was no reason why Our Mam should not have a new dress once in a blue moon. May the People's Desire to Achieve Stability by Applying Marxist Thinking Be Quickly Realised.

Resolved: to pop down to the Doves of Everlasting Peace Cut-Price Shop and see what they are asking for them flowered poplin pinafore dresses what they have in the window.

Our Gran, after declaring that the high tide of social transformation would soon sweep over the whole country, admitted that she had been guilty of revisionist tendencies. She had fancied Bakewell Tart in the 3.30 at Kempton Park, contrary to the teachings of Our Dad which were that he had seen better horses being carted into the People's Sausage Factory. She now wished to confess her recidivism and in future would back nothink but the favourite. Only thus could the proletariat be triumphant in its ceaseless struggle towards an ideological society. On the other hand, Our Gran's back was playing her up somethink awful. She could not sleep and had got this stabbing pain that started in her hands and went all up her arms and round her shoulders, she blamed that pork chop she had for her tea last night, it was all gristle. A thousand years of peace to the People's Democracy.

Resolved: to get some more of that liniment.

Our Noreen's husband Barry, in suggesting that the family collective should be even more vigilant in its efforts to avoid the corrosive influence of so-called Liberalism, asked Our Dad if he was dropping the hint that he should leave the bike out in the back garden in future. If so, he could tell Our Dad for nothink that the reactionary elements and enemies of the people at No. 43 would have it away before you could say Mao Tse-Tung. He had said nothing before as he did not want to cause trouble, but if you asked him anythink Our Dad did not know the first thing about the correct handling of contradictions among the working-class cadres, in fact he did not know his arse from his elbow. Goodwill towards the Annual National Congress of the Cultural Committee of the Communist Party, and stuff the whole lot of you.

Resolved: that our Noreen's husband Barry gets his name down for a worker's flat, sharpish.

It being opening time, the meeting adjourned after singing the *Red Flag* and separating Our Dad and Our

Noreen's husband Barry in the interests of greater understanding.

Long live the Kosycot family collective.

Down with the running jackals at No. 43.

4. Departmental ditties

Hold the back page

Colonel Benjamin Adekunle, commandant of the Nigerian
ports authority, told a press conference that a lot of the
emergency food supplies sent into his country during the
civil war was 'junk—stuff like condensed milk, canned
peaches, apricots and breakfast cereal. If it had been yams
or cassava it would have been different.' One of his peace-
time problems had been to dispose of it as it was cluttering
up valuable warehouse space.

—*The Times*

I'd been Lobby Correspondent of *Exchange and Mart* for
only six months when, early in 1950, a memo came down
from the Editor.

It was headed 'Personal announcement—1/6 for 12
words' and it read: 'Lunch! Lunch! Lunch! Editor wishes
meet Lobby Corr., Boardroom, 12.45 for 1.0. Reply in confidence, Box (London) 3649.'

It was gratifying to me that the Great Man had noticed
me at last, for I flattered myself that I had been doing well
in a quiet way. I had made the Miscellaneous Wants
column more than once, and lately one of my Whitehall
contacts had put me on to a good story about ex-Ministry
of Supply tarpaulin sheeting. The sub-editors had rewritten
my copy and put it under Household Requirements without a byline; nevertheless it was an important scoop over

Dalton's Weekly, and I was beginning to be talked about in the Press Club.

The Editor ordered US Navy-type-issue oysters and a bottle of Left Luggage Office '44, and in typically direct fashion got down to business.

'Hetherington is past it,' he said, 'I'm putting him on the Motoring Accessories desk and I want you to take over his job immediately.'

I crumbled a slice of fire-clearance-sale brown bread and tried to hide my elation. J. K. Hetherington was possibly the most distinguished war correspondent *Exchange and Mart* had ever had. His dispatches from Tobruk, when he reported brilliantly on the first-ever cache of reconditioned desert boots, radio valves and ex-Government intercommunication sets with Morse tappers in cabinets, set the fashion on war-surplus stories for years to come. But lately he'd been slipping. On his last assignment to Singapore he'd been badly beaten by Sam 'Small-ad' Peterson of the *Weekly Advertiser*, the first Western correspondent to realise that mosquito-netting could be sold as curtain material.

The Editor ordered bankrupt-stock coffee. 'Well, laddie —are you up to the job?'

'I'll do my best, sir.'

Forty-eight hours later I was in Korea. I was lucky enough to arrive on the very day that the Green Howards captured a massive dump of compasses, binoculars and telescopic sights as used by the Red Army. The story was splashed on page one at display rates and my name was made.

I covered many campaigns and travelled thousands of miles in search of a good story. I was in Cyprus for the agreement between Makarios and the British Government that was to release 10,000 RAF heavy quality greatcoats to East End warehouses. I walked, unaccompanied, down the parachute-silk road to Samarkand. When Neil Armstrong reached for the moon I got the story behind the story—the release of two million slightly sub-standard fire extinguishers from Cape Kennedy.

October 1970 found me in Lagos with little to do but wait and see what an arms deal with South Africa would produce in the way of ex-Naval gumboots. I was in the Overseas Press Club having a quiet daiquiri with Ken McAvoy, who writes the brilliant Business Opportunities column in the *Cleveland Plain Wrapper*, when a boy brought in a cable. It was from my foreign desk in London.

BADLY BEATEN LONDON TIMES STOP SURPLUS CONDENSED MILK CANNED PEACHES APRICOTS BREAKFAST CEREAL CLUTTERING NIGERIAN WAREHOUSES STOP UPFOLLOW SPEEDIEST FULLEST

It was too late at night to check the report at source. Luckily McAvoy had already made his own inquiries and had filed the story to his own paper. He owed me a favour —I'd let him in on a duffle-coat exclusive when we sweated out the Six-day War together—and so he allowed me to take a glance at his dispatch.

All I could do for the time being was re-jig McAvoy's copy and hope for a follow-up the next morning. I was taking a risk in not checking the story—but the front page was waiting.

I rolled a cable form into my reconditioned portable and tapped out:

'Bargains, bargains, bargains! Tinned food, tinned food, tinned food! Condensed milk, canned peaches, apricots, breakfast cereals etc.—unwanted, highest offer secures. Must sacrifice to clear warehouse space. Or would exchange for yams and cassava. Write Box (Lagos) 432.'

Early the next day McAvoy and I strolled round to Government House to seek an interview with Colonel Benjamin Adekunle. 'The Black Scorpion' as he is known was not there, but one of his aides was, and he was literally dancing with rage. The influential *Lagos Advertiser and Matrimonial Bulletin* had picked up McAvoy's dispatch and splashed it under the headline: 'MISCELLANEOUS SALES—THE PEOPLE MUST KNOW!'

Adekunle's aide had already prepared an official statement. The story was a canard, a fiction. If we had studied the London *Times* report in its proper context, we would have realised that none of this canned junk remained in the Nigerian warehouses. Nigeria was growing all the food it needed and had no use for canned junk. All the canned junk had been given to the International Red Cross.

I sprinted down to the Western Union office and cabled 'KILL STORY.' But it was too late. The *Exchange and Mart* had already rushed out a special edition with my story in a bargain square at bold-type rates. Seven hundred replies had already been received; thousands more must have been in the post.

I packed my canvas grip as used by Canadian officers and flew straight back to London. The office car, 23,000 miles on clock, one owner only, was not waiting at Heathrow—an ominous sign.

The editor was running his eye over the Pets (Aquarium) column when I walked into his office.

'The lad who does this stuff is very bright,' he said. 'I'd like to give him a chance to flex his muscles. How do you feel about taking over the Motoring Accessories desk from Hetherington?'

Office politics

As Personnel Records will confirm, I have been in the employ of this Company man and boy for twenty-five years, so I feel I owe a word of explanation as to why I am about to do myself in during the firm's time. Also, why I am writing this suicide note—copies to Mng Director, Sales Supervisor, Coroner, Wife, Accounts Dept and Personnel Records—on the firm's letterhead. This latter act, as I hope to make clear, is symbolic.

We must go back to the Brown Envelopes Scandal of 1963 to understand the workings of my deranged mind. Mr. Jefferson's memo to all depts, dated 4/9/63, refers. In that memo—or ultimatum, as some of us preferred to call it—Mr. Jefferson, then newly jumped-up as Stationery Supervisor, laid down that in the interests of standardisation the three sizes of white manilla envelope then in use were to be called in, and 9in by 4in brown envelopes henceforth employed for all purposes.

There were various reactions to this edict. A majority of what we might call 'company men' simply toed the party line and returned their white envelopes to stores forthwith. The bolshie element seized the opportunity to carry off white envelopes wholesale in briefcase or sandwich-box. The drifters among us merely ignored the order, using brown or white envelopes as the fit took them.

There was, however, a strong splinter group, centred mainly here in the after-sales dept, which queried the whole thinking behind Jefferson's decision. What, we asked, would happen to the white envelopes after they had been called in? Would they be sold as waste paper or would they, as some of us suspected, be left to rot in a basement storage cupboard like the wartime economy labels which are now all stuck together and unfit for use?

It was clear to me that Jefferson had not followed his policy through. I did not object to brown envelopes in any way, form or shape whatsoever; that I wish to put on record. But if we were to move into a brown envelope era, surely the transition could have been effected gradually *as and when the white envelopes were used up.*

I admit that insofar as I had any authority in after-sales —I was at that time No. 2 to Ponsonby—I encouraged the staff here to continue using white envelopes until supplies ran down. In so doing I fell foul of Ponsonby's then secretary, Miss Hopkinshaw, who was strictly in favour of playing the Jefferson memo by the book. Miss Hopkinshaw and I had already crossed swords over an electric kettle in the filing cabinet; it was not a happy time for me.

We now come to the events of 1970, and it is necessary to sketch in the background of that fateful year. Ponsonby has had his heart attack and I have stepped into his shoes; Davenport has retired, leaving a vacancy as sales director which is filled by Moody. Jefferson, to the general astonishment, takes Moody's place in Admin. Otterby takes over from Jefferson. Meanwhile Miss Hopkinshaw has also been ascending the ladder—we will not ask how. No longer a secretary but now a personal assistant, she throws in her lot with Jefferson. Thus it was that the Jefferson-Hopkinshaw axis was already lined up against me when the Hatstand Crisis of June 1970 split the office in two.

The Hatstand Crisis had its roots in the historic decision to turn the sales floor into one great office on the open-plan system. That particular bone of contention has already been well-gnawed; suffice it to say that when walls had been pulled down and partitions carted away, the office was seen to be dotted with hatstands. What had previously been private prerequisites were now public impedimenta; the hatstands had been pitched into the arena of controversy.

The after-sales staff were evenly divided: between those who did not wear hats and those who did wear hats; between those who slung their raincoats over a chair and those who had been brought up to look after their clothes properly; between those who tripped over the hastands and those who had the elementary sense to look where they were going.

For my part, I was in favour of compromise. I argued powerfully in favour of stacking the hatstands in groups of six at various strategic points around the office, where their sheer bulk would discourage further accidents. Failing that, why not range the hatstands along the wall, out of harm's way? Let reason prevail.

At the end of the day, I was unable to sway my colleagues. I recall a colourful phrase of my No. 2, Gomersall, on the day he sprained his ankle. I will not repeat it here, but it was to the effect that the hatstands should be disposed of. Very well: I would compromise further. Let the hatstands be removed on *condition that the management provide us with hooks and coathangers.*

I should stress that this was strictly an internal issue, and one which I had every confidence we in after-sales could solve among ourselves, given time. What I did not bargain for was that Gomersall was a near-neighbour of Jefferson's. That Gomersall inspired the Jefferson memo of 11/6/70 I have no doubt at all; they were seen in a public house together the evening before. Jefferson had but recently taken over in Admin, and he would have seized eagerly on the hatstand issue as a means of making his presence felt, as well as persecuting me personally.

The 11/6/70 memo spelled the kiss of death for hatstands. They were, pronounced Jefferson, an anomaly in an open-plan office. They had to go.

If he thought I proposed to lock horns with him on such a peripheral issue, he was mistaken. I 'played it cool'. As my memo of 17/6/70 (copy attached) makes clear, I agreed to Jefferson's proposals on the understanding that the management would provide the hooks and coat-hangers already mooted in my informal discussions with the after-sales staff.

Jefferson countered this ploy with the notorious memo of 18/6/70—composed, as I happen to know, by his side-kick Miss Hopkinshaw. 'My only concern is to remove the hatstands, which have become a hazard,' he wrote. 'As far as this department is concerned, you may have all the hooks and coat-hangers your heart desires, but it just so happens these are a matter for Maintenance, which is i/c office stores, and not for Admin.'

I had him in the palm of my hand. For if hooks and coat-hangers were the responsibility of Maintenance, it followed as surely as night follows day that *so were hatstands*. Jefferson had no authority whatever to remove those hatstands. Nevertheless, in a spectacular early-morning coup the next day, that is precisely what he did. My memo dated 19/6/70, copy to Mng Director, refers.

It is not for me to speculate on the relationship between Miss Hopkinshaw and the Managing Director. All I can say is that before the week was out it was made known that Maintenance, hitherto responsible for hooks, coat-hangers and hatstands, was to be brought under the umbrella of Admin. So were Staff Catering, Welfare and—more significantly—Stationery Supplies. Jefferson's empire-building had begun in earnest.

Of the Carbon Paper Affair of 1972 I will say nothing. The change from blue to black carbon paper was ostensibly Otterby's initiative, but I think I recognise the hand behind it. When Otterby had his nervous breakdown this month, Jefferson and his lackey Miss Hopkinshaw came into the open. A memo (pp Jefferson, but signed in his absence by Miss so-called Hopkinshaw) instructed all departmental heads that a multi-use internal envelope was henceforth to be used for internal memoranda. The practice of using office envelopes, that is to say the brown 9in by 4in issue as authorised on 4/9/63, was to cease. And so we had come full circle.

But there was more. The unauthorised practice of using office letterheads for internal correspondence, instead of the standard memorandum form that may be obtained by application in the first instance to Mr. Bighead Jefferson, was also discouraged. Furthermore—I am referring now to a private memo from Jefferson, though not, I may say, written on any standard memorandum form, far from it— any further rumours which I may spread about him and Miss Hopkinshaw and their activities in the night safe, although admittedly not in office hours, would lead to serious repercussions.

I was in a cleft stick, and still am. Beaten by the system, I am too old to seek another post. I certainly cannot carry on as Head of after-sales. I therefore tender my resignation on this, the office letterhead of the company. The Welfare Dept, under the aegis of Mr. Jefferson, will find me hanging from the Advance Towel Supply unit in the No. 4 cloakroom. It is my last wish that the Managing Director may be present, so that he may observe at first hand the state of that cloakroom since Jefferson took over.

Passing of the third-floor buck

The Office Relations Bill, published yesterday by the Department of Employment, begins by setting out three general principles with the purpose of promoting good office relations.

The first principle is that an office is not a tea-bar, matrimonial bureau, betting shop, reading room, fashion house or smoking lounge, but a place where paperwork necessary to good management is originated and eventually filed.

The second principle is that the paperwork referred to in the first principle should be filed in the right place. The Bill points out that it, the Bill, would have been published six months ago had earlier drafts been filed under O for Office and not used as table-mats at Miss Tibbotson's leaving-party.

The third principle deals perfunctorily with freedom and security for office workers, including those who are manifestly incapable of writing their own names.

Clause 1 of the Bill sets out the general principles with a short addendum on certain goings-on behind the filing cabinets of the Department of Employment, which have got to stop.

Clause 2 makes void the office worker's right, or what the office worker fondly imagines is a right, to take home vast stocks of typing paper, envelopes, ball-point pens, gummed labels and the remainder. It contains provisions for setting the dog on whoever it is keeps taking the Minister's pencils.

Clause 3 requires whoever it is who makes daisy-chains out of the paper-clips to unpick them.

Clause 4 obliges the office-boy to stop whistling in the corridors.

Clause 5 provides for a fair standard rate in respect of office collections. It lays down the following maximum scales by which employees may be mulcted of funds for useless presents:

For a female employee leaving to get married, fifty pence.

For a male ditto, twenty-five pence.

For a 21st birthday celebration comprising green Chartreuse all round for the typing pool, five pence.

For a colleague lolling about in hospital with a broken leg acquired during a ski-ing holiday, two and a half pence.

For floral tributes at the funeral of the office boy's grandmother, nothing.

Clause 6 reduces the number of hours in which an office worker may skulk in the lavatory.

Clause 7 limits the employee's practice of using the telephone as his own private property. This clause has special reference to Mr. Bates of Forward Planning and his girl friend in Norway.

Clause 8 is a sustained piece of invective against the Department of Employment typing pool. It contains provisions for the entire typing pool to have their heads dipped in a bucket of cold water three times a day.

Clause 9 makes it an unfair office practice to barge into an employer's office whining about the central heating or lack of it, the state of the ladies' rest room, the shortage of carbon paper, the possession by any employee of only one pair of hands, or the groping activities of Mr. Bates of Forward Planning.

Clause 10 provides for the instant dismissal of Mr. Bates of Forward Planning.

Clause 11 defines and standardises certain terms and

expressions with the object of improving the smooth flow of

'Nine a.m.' means not half past nine, not a quarter past nine, not five past nine, but nine a.m.

'Now' means now.

'Three copies' means three copies, ie not the original and two copies.

'Tell me, Miss Hopcraft, do you have difficulty in understanding what I'm saying?' means than an employer's instructions have not been followed.

'Inform Mr. Bates of Forward Planning that I want him off the premises in ten minutes, otherwise I shall call the police' means that members of the Forward Planning department are drinking whisky out of tea-cups.

Clause 12 defines the circumstances in which an employer is entitled to use foul language towards Miss Hopcraft. Paramount among these is Miss Hopcraft's habit of typing urgent memoranda with the carbon paper inserted the wrong way round.

Clause 13 allocates responsibility for tea being served up slopped in the saucer.

Clause 14 establishes a procedure for transferring Miss Hopcraft to Bournemouth.

Clause 15 empowers an employer to require a ballot where he is satisfied that office sweepstakes are being run in an atmosphere of coercion, undue persuasion or downright blackmail. Where an employee of a junior grade has been induced to buy tickets in excess of the value of £5 (five pounds) from an employee of a senior grade, an employer is entitled to ask where he, the employee of a junior grade, got the money.

Clause 16 limits the circulation during office time of jokes concerning the travelling salesman, the farmer, the farmer's wife, the pig, and the farmer's squint-eyed daughter.

Clause 17 limits, or come to think of it totally prohibits, the office Christmas party.

Clause 18 enables Miss Hopcraft either to get herself

off to Bournemouth and stop snivelling, or to take advantage of the early retirement scheme.

Clause 19 establishes the right of all office workers to cultivate rubber plants, knit, read detective fiction, manicure their nails, discuss last night's television programmes, write personal letters, complete crosswords, or play pontoon, hangman, knock-knock and that game involving a screwed-up ball of paper and two rulers, always provided that these activities are pursued in the office workers' own time and on their own premises.

Clause 20 requires Miss Hopcraft and Mr. Bates of Forward Planning to come out of the stationery cupboard forthwith.

Virgins for industry

What, exactly, are the aims and purpose of Virgins for Industry?

The aims and purpose of Virgins for Industry are, foremost, to restore British virginity to its former prestigious position in the markets of the world; secondly, to impress upon young men and women the economic and social advantages of retaining their virginity before it is too late; thirdly to rid Government, Industry and the Trade Union Movement of dangerous non-virgin elements whose avowed objective is to establish Great Britain as the Sodom and Gomorrah of Western Europe; and fourthly to campaign unceasingly for the removal of the iniquitous Tax on Virginity.

Is Virgins for Industry, then, a political organisation?

Virgins for Industry is completely unpolitical. We believe, however, that the present trend towards permissiveness is directly traceable to the folly of socialist politicians who publicly admit to being active non-virgins. We also believe that millions of man-hours are being lost each year as the result of lust and fornication on the factory floor, as well as behind filing cabinets. It is our contention that only a Virgin Government can lead Britain back to strength, chastity and economic sanity.

Virgins for Industry was recently accused by a Socialist

*Member of Parliament of being interested only in increased
production and profits at the cost of other people's pleasure.
Is there any truth in this scurrilous libel?*

The socialist politician who made this vicious and cow-
ardly attack under the cover of Parliamentary privilege is,
it is openly admitted, the father of two children. Thus he
publicly flaunts his confession that he has been in bed with
a woman on at least two occasions. Were he to present himself at the House of Commons with a mattress strapped on
his back, it could not be a clearer indictment of his direct
interest in the permissive lobby.

But let us examine these groundless allegations. What is
this so-called 'pleasure' which it is said we seek to deny the
British people? Let us make no bones about it, it is the
'pleasure' of sex— which, as many doctors have testified,
leads *directly* to rape, incest, abortion, prostitution, venereal
diseases, adultery, illegitimacy, nervous exhaustion and like
perils.

And who really wants this 'pleasure'? Not, you may be
assured, the Virgins of Britain. No virgin lathe operator
ever approaches the foreman for half a day off so that he
may defend himself in a sordid paternity suit. No virgin
secretary fails to turn up at her desk because she is suffering from morning sickness. We do not see virgin company
directors ashen-faced with worry, and unable to deal with
important export orders, because some woman has just
rung up to say that she must see them at once, and it's very
urgent.

No, the British virgin is happy to forego such 'pleasures.'

*Other critics, with the best of motives, claim that Virgins
for Industry is impracticable. They say that if we were all
practising Virgins, Britain would be uninhabited within
seventy years.*

Certainly there would be a marked decline in the demand
for subsidised housing, free education and other perquisites
of the Welfare State which (since the Exchequer does not

look kindly on the single man) are largely paid for by the iniquitous Tax on Virginity.

But it is wrong to say that Virgins for Industry is reaching for the moon. We are realists, and we recognise that there must always be an unhappy minority who will indulge in sexual intercourse, just as there will always be drug-addicts, alcoholics, perverts and criminals. However, just as we would not expect to be governed by drug-addicts, alcoholics, perverts and criminals, neither do we wish to be governed by those who indulge in the sexual act.

You have convinced me that criticism of Virgins for Industry is either ill-formed or malicious. Now, speaking constructively, could you outline the economic advantages of virginity which you mentioned earlier?

Even allowing for the iniquitous Tax on Virginity, the practising Virgin earning, say, £2,000 a year, is many times better off than his fornicating opposite number. Here is one case from among hundreds on our files.

As a *direct result* of losing his virginity at the age of twenty-three, John B., a chartered accountant living in Middlesex, is now the father of three girls under the age of twelve. Having kept careful records of his expenditure he has been able to calculate that the cost of his brood in the way of clothes, food, shelter, education, birthday and Christmas presents, toys, holidays, horse-riding lessons. Brownie uniforms, soft drinks, sweets, ice-cream, pocket money, subscriptions to *Jackie* and the remainder, has so far amounted to the fantastic sum of £10,700.

By remaining a Virgin a young man of equivalent income would be able to *save* £10,700 within twelve years.

You might have added that such a sum when invested would actually appreciate over this period. But money is not everything. What are the social advantages of virginity?

An independent survey has shown that the Virgin has *twenty-five times* more leisure than a non-virgin. Leisure in which to read improving books. Leisure to take up a rewarding and profitable hobby such as coin-collecting. Leisure to peruse the correspondence course that may rocket him to the top of his profession. He is also, from the employment point of view, a more efficient working unit, far less likely than the non-virgin to arrive at desk or work-bench with circles around his eyes, waste precious hours mooning about in the typing pool, or write pornographic letters on the firm's stationery. Remember, too, that it is the Virgin with *twenty-five* times more leisure at his disposal who is best able to serve his country in Government at all its levels.

Twenty-five times more leisure! Surely this is a stagger-ing figure which will come as a revelation to all thinking men and women?

It is indeed a staggering figure, and one that perhaps deserves to be explained in a little more detail. Our argu-ment, which is based not on theory but on fact, is that the average Virgin is, hour for hour, twenty-five times more productive than the average non-virgin, irrespective of the quality, use or desirability of that which is being produced.

Time-and-motion studies show that for every fifteen minutes spent in copulation by a non-virgin, *five hours* is consumed in preparatory activities such as bathing, dress-ing, applying after-shave lotion and other unguents, drink-ing cocktails, dining by candlelight, dancing, groping in taxi-cabs and professing a mutual interest in certain gramo-phone records. Even then the end-product—such as it is— is not guaranteed.

In a comparable period, a Virgin who has decided to spend his evening sorting through his collection of day-of-issue stamps will not have wasted a single minute. Nor, according to independent costings, will he have incurred a restaurant bill for £8.55 plus fifteen per cent tip.

It is clear that sex is wasteful, time-consuming, expensive and that there is no place for it in modern Britain. How do you propose to drive this message home?

By disseminating literature such as this in schools, youth clubs, offices and factories. By setting fire to hotel beds. By spreading rumours that the Pill causes women to grow moustaches. By patrolling Hampstead Heath shouting 'Disgusting filth!' at courting couples. By discouraging office parties. By taking a full-page announcement in *The Times* newspaper denouncing HM Government as lechers and fornicators.

Naturally, all this costs money, and we exist entirely on voluntary subscriptions. We rely on *your* support.

I would like to join Virgins for Industry. How do I set about becoming a virgin?

An embarrassing year

The annual general meeting of Foolhardy Enterprises was held on November 18, 1969, in London, the chairman and managing director presiding. The following is his statement circulated with the annual report and accounts for the year ended April 30, 1969.

It has been, I regret to inform this meeting of shareholders, another disappointing year for your company. The Chancellor's inflexible and to some minds unimaginative policy of tighter money, the inevitable trade fluctuations of a downward nature following devaluation, and the continued attraction of the Deutschmark coupled with the death from food poisoning of the racing greyhound Can She Do It, in which your company had a substantial holding, have all been contributory factors.

It will be observed that the balance sheet shows a net loss over the financial year of some £800 sterling. These adverse figures reflect a deficit representing as to £150 carried forward from the Small Night Club in Basildon New Town Account, of which I am unhappy to inform shareholders that they have not yet heard the last; £75 written off in respect of the racing greyhound Can She Do It; and as to £575 representing depreciation as regards new investments contracted in accordance with your board's policy of diversification and re-entrenchment.

It is with the warmest pleasure that I am able to welcome your board's brother-in-law Percy to this annual general meeting. If you will consult the circulated accounts under the heading 'Assets' you will see that one item—indeed, it is the only item under this particular heading—refers to an investment of £200 in the expanding field of bistro-type restaurants. Notwithstanding your company's previously unsatisfactory ventures into the catering market, we were sufficiently impressed by the prospectus of your board's brother-in-law Percy as to stake all your company's present assets in the goodwill and freehold of a basement restaurant to be named 'Percy's Pantry' in the vicinity of the King's Road, Chelsea. Your company's participation in this venture will attract first call on five per cent of the net profits after certain debts have been paid; a survey of similar establishments in this important location would suggest that an annual turnover in the order of £20,000 rising to £100,000 per annum may be anticipated. Nor will these be the only benefits accruing to your company. Plans are already in hand for a programme of phased development that will embrace initially a second 'Percy's Pantry' in Hampstead, the probability of a 'Percy's Other Pantry' two doors from the parent establishment, and the eventual ploughing-back of surplus profits into the as yet under-realised field of coin-operated fruit-pie dispensing machines in key positions throughout the West End. I have the personal assurance of your board's brother-in-law that your company will be invited to participate in all these challeng-ing and forward-looking ventures on a basis of complete parity.

Turning now to the technical loss which your company has sustained on paper during the last year of trading, I would refer first of all to the discouraging results so far shown by our revitalised entertainments division. Share-holders will recall that in recent years your board has stead-fastly declined to put the company's capital at risk in the musical entertainments *Hair*, *Fiddler on the Roof* and *Forty Years On* on the grounds that they would not run. A thorough investigation of this area of investment, how-ever, suggested that the commercial theatre was now on firmer ground, that it was slowly recovering from the swingeing blow of SET to which I referred last year in respect of our failure to make headway in the promising arena of small night clubs in Basildon New Town, and that this important market was ripe for exploitation. Accordingly your board felt able to authorise a sum of not more than £100 to be annexed by the General Fund representing as to a year's option on a musical adaptation of Plato's *Republic*, the book and lyrics of which were written by your board's sister's little girl's piano teacher.

It would be fruitless to conjecture at this late date what might have been the return in terms of capital, trips to the Bahamas and the remainder had Mr. Richard Burton and Mr. Rex Harrison been able to accept the generous offer that was made to them to play the leading parts in this entertainment. It is now no longer a matter of private confidence that they had a prior commitment to the film *Staircase* (in which your company has no financial interest), and your company's option on the property has now lapsed. The additional item of £3 under this general heading is in respect of entertainment to a man called Simpson, who said that he could get your company into show business.

It may be that a word of amplification is called for in respect of the item 'Goldfish, £250,' under the general heading 'Complete Write-off.' In November of last year your company was approached on behalf of a small firm trading under the name of London Goldfish Boutique Ltd. The chairman of London Goldfish, as well as being a member of the Can She Do It consortium, was also known to your board by virtue of having occupied an adjoining bedspace when your board was in the Royal Signals. This in itself seemed a powerful argument for linking our capital and know-how with the fortunes of London Goldfish. Other points were forcibly made: that there was no other goldfish boutique operating in the metropolitan area, that valuable trade was being lost by the company having to trade from a barrow in Berwick Street market rather than in permanent premises, and that an investment of £250 would, after overheads had been covered, yield a return of between £10 and £15 a week in crumpled notes. Regrettably, the end of the trading year saw the chairman of London Goldfish behind bars for passing cheques while still an undischarged bankrupt, and the anticipated growth of this holding did not take place.

May I now touch on our obligations *vis-à-vis* the Small Night Club in Basildon New Town situation? It will be recalled that in 1958 your company entered into partnership with your board's cousin Alfie who had been managing director of our fish-and-chip shop interests until on the advice of our bankers we withdrew from the competitive field of fried comestibles. Your board's cousin, it will be recollected, put very strikingly the proposition that no small night club existed in Basildon New Town; he envisaged the day when there would be not one but three, and on that basis your company agreed to capitalise the venture in consideration of 50 per centum of the ordinary shares. Our interest in this property should normally have lapsed on the quarter-day following the prosecution of the club for mounting cabarets of a lewd and disgusting nature. It transpires, however, that since the closure of the club your board's cousin Alfie has been roaming about the country drawing cheques on the Small Night Club in Basildon Account. I fear that pending official winding-up proceedings our commitments in this unproductive area may be spectacular.

The figures £5, £10, £15, £20, £25, £50 and £75 under 'Sundry losses' represent an experimental policy of escalating investment in connection with the racing greyhound Can She Do It before that animal was written off. The figure £7 represents a hedging bet on the racing greyhound Come On Pete. The figure £22 represents your Board's floating investment in Littlewood's Pools Ltd. The item 'Nil' under 'Profits' is self explanatory.

The progress your company has achieved in the past year would have been encouraging but for the adverse trading climate then prevailing. I am convinced that the economic barometer is now set fair, and that the winds of fortune will blow us to well-deserved prosperity in 1970.

The thirteenth floor and other stories

Achievement House is one of those 'prestige' office blocks on the western fringes of the City. If the reader has ever tried to find St. Paul's Cathedral he may have noticed the dome and portico reflecting prettily in its glass façade. It is the last place where one would expect an adventure in the supernatural. And yet, and yet ...

In 1968 I was left a little money by my grandfather and resolved in consequence to go into business on my own account as an importer of tobacco and snuff. Such experience as I had had in this direction—I had for many years sold cigarettes from a kiosk near Liverpool Street Station—suggested that Achievement House would be the ideal location for my activities. As well as being convenient for the docks, Customs House and No. 11 bus it was, as I have said, a 'prestige' address—of no small importance when one is dealing with businessmen of the calibre of Messrs. W. D. and H. O. Wills or Rothman of Pall Mall. The thirteenth floor, I happened to know, was completely vacant, indeed had been advertised as such at a rent per square foot well within my recently-enhanced means.

The agents for Achievement House were no other than Messrs. Hardwicke and Hardwicke of Lower Regent Street. I knew Mr. Terence, the senior partner, well—many and many is the time I have served him an ounce of Gold Flake from my little kiosk—and he readily volunteered to accompany me on an inspection of the premises. In the event, however, he was ill with influenza, and his son Mr. Jonathan being engaged upon other business, I was handed a bunch of keys by a clerk and sallied forth alone to Achievement House.

My somewhat shabby appearance must have contrasted oddly with the opulence of my surroundings, and so I thought little of the Commissionaire's strange look as he ushered me into the lift, nor of the inquisitive glance of the lift's only other occupant—an office boy by the look of him—as I emerged at the thirteenth floor. Yet at the same time I felt a shiver of apprehension—some small presentiment that all was not as it should have been.

What I expected at the thirteenth floor I hardly knew, beyond the indisputable fact that I had been given an order to view some two thousand square feet of unoccupied space. I was certainly not prepared to find my 'empty' offices in the hands of an apparently thriving firm of public relations advisers. Yet such was indubitably the case. The main door let upon a reception area which also served as a typing pool. Here perhaps a dozen girls were engaged at Remington or Gestetner. Beyond the reception area were numerous glass-partitioned booths occupied by various shirt-sleeved men—one gesticulating into a telephone, one doodling on a blotter, another working at a drawing-board.

Staring, I became aware that the receptionist was asking me to state my business. I mumbled an excuse and hurried away.

I have said that I was personally acquainted with Mr. Terence Hardwicke, the estate agent representing Achievement House. Perhaps I did not know him well enough to warrant intruding upon him at his home in Epping. But I was angry: I had been sent on a fool's errand. I am the mildest of men as a rule but I considered myself a victim of professional incompetence and I desired satisfaction. I looked up his address, telephoned for an appointment and hurried to Epping.

Mr. Terence received me in his bedroom and listened

courteously to my grievance. When I had finished he asked quietly:

'Tell me, was the man doodling on his blotter of medium height, with a small moustache?'

'I believe so,' I said shortly. 'However, I fail to see—'

Mr. Terence, with a strange look, cut me short.

'I can only imagine you are unwell,' he said, 'and that you are confusing your impression of Achievement House this morning with some previous visit to the place.'

'I swear I have never been to Achievement House before in my life.'

'Then I must inform you,' said Mr. Terence impressively, 'that the man you saw was *stabbed to death six months ago*.'

I stared. I felt in the nape of my neck the same prickly sensation I had experienced when first entering Achievement House.

'But his colleagues!' I cried. 'The man gesticulating into the telephone—another one working at a drawing board—'

'—were convicted at the Old Bailey of a particularly brutal murder. One hanged himself by his braces, the other died of a heart-attack upon hearing his sentence.'

I recalled, now, hearing something about the case. But I pride myself that I am nothing if not level-headed. It could well have been that Mr. Terence, an astute businessman with an eye to the main chance, had his own reasons for discouraging me from the leasehold of the thirteenth floor.

'An interesting story,' I remarked. 'But one which does not account for *the presence of the typing pool*!'

Mr. Terence gave a short, bitter laugh.

'You simple fool! Why do you think you were offered those offices as such an advantageous rent? The place is cursed! You speak of the typing pool—about a dozen girls, I believe?'

'There would have been about a dozen.'

'The first, Joyce Benson, drowned herself after an unhappy love affair. A second, Hetty Wilkinson, threw herself off London Bridge after the death of her closest friend. A third, fourth, fifth, and sixth, Miss Parkinson, Mrs. Dougall and the sisters Parrish all expired from food poisoning at an office Christmas party. A seventh, eighth, ninth, tenth, eleventh, and twelfth—'

At this point I felt a hand on my shoulder. I turned and found myself gazing into the grim countenance of Mr. Jonathan, the junior partner.

'May I ask what you are doing in my house?'

'I—why, Mr. Jonathan, I am here at your father's invitation!' (I had not yet noticed that the older man had unobtrusively left the room.)

Mr. Jonathan gave me a strange look.

'When was this?'

'Why—not an hour ago. On the telephone.'

'That is impossible. *My father has been dead these three months past!*'

I tell you, I was out of that house in an instant. I know not where I fled. I must have walked about for a time and then taken a train, for presently I found myself sitting in my club, the Junior Sycophant in Dover Street. It was still early and Jorkins was the only member present. He is an unsympathetic fellow and there is no love lost between us, but I had to unburden myself or burst. I told Jorkins my tale.

He was silent for some time, gripping the arms of his wing chair and staring into the fire. Presently he said:

'Tell me, did you actually see Jonathan Hardwicke enter the room?'

'I don't believe I did. Why do you ask?'

Jorkins gave me a strange look.

'I only ask,' said he, 'because Jonathan Hardwicke *committed suicide the day after his father's death*. Some trouble over the books, I believe.'

I sat, open-mouthed, my head spinning. How long I sat thus I cannot say. I noticed that the club porter had entered and was putting logs on the fire.

'Something wrong, sir?'

'Wrong, Pearson? What should be wrong?' I asked sharply.

'I was only a-wondering, sir. I thought as 'ow I heard you talking—and then I see'd as 'ow you was all alone.'

It was true. The wing chair opposite me was empty. I cried:

'But what about the gentleman who was here—?'

The porter looked at me strangely.

'Gentleman, sir? There's been no one else in the club this last 'alf-hour or more.'

And there my story would end, but for the circumstance that my grandfather calls at my kiosk each Tuesday for his ounce of Navy Mixture. It was Tuesday the following day and I told him of my strange encounter at the Junior Sycophant. When I finished my grandfather reminded me, gently, that the Junior Sycophant Club had been pulled down a year previously.

'Besides,' he added with a strange look, 'you seem to have forgotten that it was only because of the inheritance you received *as a result of my death* that this whole absurd imbroglio first began.'

Then he vanished, and I was left alone in my little kiosk, which, now that I remember, burned down, and me in it, over a year ago.

What my tale proves I do not pretend to know. Are things always what they seem? Is the past somehow engaged with the present, or the present with the future? Or is there some rational explanation for the events of that day? Perhaps the reader, when he has put this copy of *John O' London's Weekly* aside, may reach his own conclusions.

A star is born Ltd

The London Palladium and other Moss Empires Theatres in London and the provinces are to be leased for business conferences, press shows, sales meetings and the like.
—*Financial Times*

It was in the early nineteen-seventies that I got my first big break—a solo spot in the second half of the British Exporters' Working Lunch at the London Palladium. And what a break it turned out to be! 'A star overnight!' crowed the *Financial Times*. 'Has that indefinable magic of the truly dedicated performer,' said the *Economist*. 'A hit, a palpable hit!' screamed *The Times Business News*. 'Another Lord Mancroft—the days of greatness are back in the British music hall,' was the verdict of the *Stock Exchange Gazette*.

I was flattered by this ovation—what stage-struck youngster wouldn't be? And the offers were already pouring in. Could I take over the ICI spot at the Talk of the Town? Would I appear with British Petroleum at the Desert Inn, Las Vegas? Was I available for a special guest appearance on the Lloyds Bank Unit Trust Spectacular on Thames-TV?

It was the big time and no mistake, when you consider that only a week before I had been playing to half-empty houses in a touring-company production of the Builders', Glaziers' and Roofing-tile Manufacturers' Sales Conference. But although I was cock-a-hop at reaching the West End, and grateful to the critics for their generous 'quotes', I couldn't help but feel peeved at being hailed as their latest 'discovery.' A star overnight, was I? Did they know how long I'd worked and slaved for this moment? Had they any idea how many years of heartbreak and shattered hopes a businessman has to endure before he finally sees his name in lights?

I suppose, in a way, I was luckier than some, for I was 'born in a trunk' as the saying is, and grew up with no illusions about the so-called glamour of business life. My father was George Upchurch of Upchurch, Nephew and Patterson (Brake Linings) Ltd., who used to play the old Salford Hippodrome with their annual general meeting. They couldn't afford a pianist at that time, and so my mother used to perch me in the orchestra pit in my high chair while she accompanied the company report. And what tough audiences they were in those days! I remember that my father and his partners worked out a hilarious bankruptcy routine. They were rewarded with salvoes of fruit from the indignant shareholders in the gallery.

After this fiasco the act was streamlined and brought up to date, and began touring the Moss Empire circuit as Upchurch, Nephew and Patterson (Chemical Fertilisers) Ltd. Things were looking good and were getting better all the time, and my father's agent was beginning to interest some of the West End managements in the act. Then Patterson, who had apparently let a rave review from the *Liverpool Post* City Page go to his head, suddenly demanded top billing. There was a bitter quarrel which culminated in the partnership breaking up, and my father decided to go solo.

It was as George Upchurch and Co., Manufacturers of Fireplaces Since 1870, that he turned up in London to try his luck. He found an 'angel' and staged his first non-stop sales conference at the Victoria Palace early in 1970. It was something new for a sophisticated West End audience, and it broke all records. Soon my father's catchphrase—
'Sod the quality, lad, get the buggers sold'—was on every

lip. I remember that we celebrated his one hundredth performance with a family supper at the Ivy. As the door-man ushered us in I saw my father toss half-a-crown to a ragged busker who was reciting some Board of Trade annual returns in the gutter. It was Patterson, who had once demanded top billing! How are the mighty fallen!

I, of course, was learning all the time. I remember vividly being taken to see the incomparable Cecil King at, I believe, a Foyle's Literary Lunch where he was doing cabaret. His big break came too late in life for a season at the Palladium, and I believe he is now playing the northern clubs. George Brown of the Courtald Follies was another all-time 'great'. I saw him in his heyday before bookings began to fall off and he had to accept dates in the Middle East. His material has grown a little thin by now perhaps, but still a great showman in my opinion.

It was taken for granted that I would one day take to the boards myself. After working as prop-boy for my father I registered my own act at Bush House—George Upchurch Junior, Scrap Metal Dealer (1970) Ltd. Although I say it as shouldn't, it wasn't a bad little act at all. I spent endless nights rehearsing in front of a mirror in my bedroom. It was a little trade show routine which I'd written myself: a fifteen-minute solo on the price of aluminium scrap, ten minutes for questions—my brother Albert was always the drunk in the audience who leaned out his box waving a cigar and asking 'What is the top quotation per pound for grade one zinc sheeting?'—and then a rousing patriotic song.

Bookings at first were few. For a while I played the commercial hotels in the Midlands—furniture exhibitions, vacuum-cleaner demonstrations, anything I could get. Then I heard that a car-insurance act had tried to work Up-church, Nephew and Patterson's old bankruptcy gag at the Blackpool Palace, and had been well and truly given the raspberry. The management needed a replacement in a hurry and I—having travelled to Blackpool on the over-night train—was on their doorstep. I was put on between

G. Sneape (Holdings) Ltd., who used to do bird imitations, and the Liberal Party Assembly. G. Sneape is now an agent who has grown prosperous with road-show productions of such evergreen favourites as the Hat Trade Annual Teach-In and the Aims of Industry Standing Press Conference. What became of the Liberal Party I don't know. Someone told me they were working the end of the pier at Llandudno. Perhaps they will make a 'comeback' one of these days.

Anyway, I seemed to click. The zinc sheeting routine went down a treat, and I took seven curtain-calls. On the strength of my success I blew my last few pounds on a first class single ticket to London.

Things were not easy, even with my father's influence. Those were the really great days of the Palladium and the Victoria Palace, and I was up against such glittering personalities as the Beecham Group, Tate and Lyle ('Just Clowning'), and Unilever, Keppell and Betty. I struggled on in semi-obscurity for a while. I did warm-ups for the Reed Paper Group. I was stand-in for Peter Cadbury for a few days. I even did walk-ons in a COI press show that closed after one night.

Then Mr. Grade happened to catch my act, at a fortuitous moment. Robert Maxwell was packing them in at the Palladium but he had had an attractive offer from New York and wanted to be released from his contract. I was auditioned and got the part. And will I ever forget the dazzling moment when, in fear and trembling, I turned up at the London Palladium and saw my name in lights among the stars:

JOHN PLAYER & SON LTD.
'Fills the stage with fags'

BRITISH NATIONAL EXPORT COUNCIL
Thrills and Spills

MASSEY-FERGUSON (UNITED KINGDOM) LTD.
'Down on the Farm'

GEORGE UPCHURCH JR., SCRAP METAL DEALER
(1970) Ltd.
'Here to amuse you'

The rest is history. A year later I was honoured to be invited to repeat my act at the Royal Command Performance, second on the bill only to the Prudential Assurance Company. I have now only one ambition left, and that is to be elected Chief Barker of the Confederation of British Industry.

The twelve days of shopping

A Pear Tree, sir? Yes, indeed, sir, we have a wide selection of pear trees. May I recommend the Jargonelle, number three in the catalogue? It bears a small green and brown tapering fruit, will succeed on a sunless wall and is resistant to scab.

Naturally we deliver, sir. If you will write down the lady's address we can guarantee that she'll get her pear tree on the first day of Christmas.

Will there be anything else, sir?

A partridge? Of course, sir. We specialise in game birds. If you would step into the Food Hall ...

Oh, I see, a *live* partridge. If we don't have one in stock we can certainly get one for you, sir.

I suppose we could find a way of attaching it to the pear tree, sir. We could probably tie its feet up with string. Or ribbon, if you'd like it gift-wrapped.

Excuse me, sir, let me be quite sure I've got your instructions clear. You want *twelve* pear trees, to be delivered on successive days?

Would you like different varieties of pear tree? Packham's Triumph? Conference? Laxton's Early Market? Very good, sir. Twelve of the Jargonelle.

And twelve live partridges.

No bother at all, sir, I assure you. I'll just make out your invoice, unless you'd like to look round at all?

Two turtle doves, sir? Ah, I've got you. *Twenty-two*

turtle doves, to be delivered in eleven batches, the first pair to arrive on the second day of Christmas.

Do you want them tied up in any particular kind of tree, sir? Bramley Seedling? Newton Wonder? Flowering cherry?

Very good, sir. No more trees.

Yes, sir, we do a very good line in French hens. They go very well with the dwarf conifers, I think you'll find. We could strap their feet to the branches and sprinkle them with glitter dust, if you so required. Highly seasonable effect, sir.

Just the French hens. As you wish, sir. Three per diem, making two and a half dozen in all. I don't know whether we've got that many in stock, sir, but we can always have them flown in for you.

If the lady's interested in bird-life, sir, we can do you a slightly shop-soiled ostrich. Or what about thirty or forty penguins?

Owls? Parrots? Oyster catchers? Snowy egrets? Laughing gulls? Vultures?

Colly birds it is, sir. A wise choice, if I may say so. I think the lady will be very pleased.

Is there anything else I can show you, sir? Fur coats? Cigarette lighters? Rare coins? Precious stones? Jewellery?

You can have as many gold rings as you wish, sir.

You wouldn't like to round it up to an even twenty-five gross, would you, sir? It would save me opening the crate.

Just as you like, sir. Five gold rings each day, delivery to commence on the fifth day of Christmas. There'll be a small extra charge for the use of the armoured car. Unless you'd care to buy it outright, sir? Many ladies are driving their own armoured cars this season.

Ah, well if the lady doesn't drive there's no point in drawing your attention to our excellent stock of Rolls-Bentleys. Would you like to see the music department, sir? Perhaps I could mix you up a few grand pianos?

Geese, sir? You mean wall plaques? Flying geese? I'm afraid the only ones we have in are the common or garden plaster of Paris variety, but we could always get our work-shop to encrust them with jewels.

I'm with you now, sir. Geese a-laying. I didn't realise we were back on live birds. Forty-two pregnant geese, first lot for delivery on the sixth day of Christmas. And you say you don't want them in trees? How about if we strung them all up on Christmas trees, sir?

You're quite right, sir, it *would* be over-doing it. Anything else in the bird line before we move on?

Swans coming up, sir.

Ah, now I'm afraid if you want them a-swimming we can't do them at the price marked on the tag. It's a special order, see, sir. We'd have to get them a garden pool apiece.

If it's no trouble to the lady, sir, it's no trouble to us, believe you me. Anything you'd like with the garden pools? Lilies? Stone frogs? Goldfish? Gnomes?

I'm sorry, sir, we don't do human beings.

Well, I suppose we could always book you some maids a-milking through an agency, but there'd be a small surcharge. Do you want the same eight to turn up each day, or were you thinking of more of a cumulative effect?

I quite agree, sir. It'll give the lady a good laugh. And we'll do the same with the lords a-leaping, the pipers piping and all the rest of the crew. Just leave it with me, sir.

I'll tell you what'd go very nicely with this lot, if you don't mind my saying, sir. Seeing the lady has a sense of humour, you want to top it all off by sending a hearse round.

A hearse, sir. Our funeral department offers a discreet and sympathetic service.

Beg pardon, sir, it was just a suggestion.

And you say you're not interested in the ostrich? What I was thinking, sir, we could wire it up in a zonking great silver birch tree. *Betula verrucosa*, sir, number six in the catalogue—very popular with the ladies. An elegant tree, requiring light porous soil with—

As you please, sir.

And will that be all, sir? Any tinned fruit, caviar, four-poster beds, light aircraft, service flats? The first battalion of the Coldstream Guards?

I'll just make out your bill, sir. Let me see now, that's one dozen Jargonelle pear trees, one dozen live partridges, twenty-two turtle doves, thirty French hens, three dozen colly birds, forty gold rings, forty-two geese a-laying, ditto swans a-swimming with matching garden pools, forty maids a-milking, three dozen ladies dancing, thirty lords a-leaping, twenty-two pipers piping and one dozen drummers drumming.

No, sir, I'm afraid we don't accept credit cards.

Please adjust your files

A firm which trades in credit information on individuals said at the weekend that it planned to be fully computerised within a year, and would have personal dossiers on 80 per cent of the country's population in 10 years' time.

—*Daily Telegraph*

To the General Manager, the Millstone Building Society.
Dear Sir,

I am sorry that you cannot find it in your heart to stake me a ninety per cent advance on £6,000-worth of bricks and mortar in the area of Bath Road, near Hounslow, Middlesex. I can well understand that having had me vetted by a firm which trades in credit information on individuals (do you pay them cash on the nail, by the way, or is your rating better than mine?) you feel doubtful that I would be able to keep up to scratch as regards the mortgage repayments. As you rightly point out, I am unemployed (actually, I think the word the computer was searching for is *self-employed*, but we'll let that pass) and it is perfectly true that I have a police record. This happens, as a matter of fact, to be nothing more sinister than an LP on the Decca label of the Metropolitan Police Dance Orchestra playing selections from *Charley Girl*, but as I paid for it by credit card I can see that there may have been some confusion when the information was fed into my friendly

164

neighbourhood I.B.M. machine.

What does pain me, however, is the gratuitous suggestion that I am an incendiary in the pay of the Russians, and that my purpose in finding a modest semi in the Bath Road area is to blow up London Airport. I think you are only creating confusion by sending copies of the letter refusing my mortgage to M.I.5., Scotland Yard, Esso Petroleum, the British Airports Authority, and particularly the firm which trades in credit information on individuals, who will undoubtedly add another black mark against my name.

I feel that I have the right to reply and would like to deal with some of the more hair-raising items on my dossier.

1. *Petroleum spirit, suspicious possession of.* It is perfectly true that during the past year I have bought petroleum spirit by cheque in great quantities. It is also true, as the computer has learned from its narks in the motor trade, that I do not own a car. It is equally true that I cannot even drive.

So what, the computer must have been asking itself, did I want with 480 gallons of petrol? Clearly it was not for the purpose of removing grease-stains from my dinner jacket, for as the computer's social correspondent has accurately reported, I have not been invited to any public function for over twelve months. I deny that this so-called ostracisation has left me with a grudge against society.

I will come clean on this issue.

The fact is (the computer can confirm this from photostats of advertisements which I have placed in *Exchange and Mart* over the years) that I am a dedicated collector of ephemera. Earlier this year I developed an obsessional interest in assembling a complete set of World Cup medallions. It is entirely due to the elusive Bobby Moore that I had to purchase so many cans of Esso Plus to make my collection complete. The petrol I sold at cut rates to a friend of mine called Beasley. This accounts for the regular payments from Beasley which appear in my bank statement. It is not true that I was blackmailing Beasley.

2. *Russian language, extensive knowledge of.* I swear

before God that I cannot speak Russian and have no interest in the Soviet Union. Where the computer is making its mistake is in its assumption that because my living room is crammed from floor to ceiling with the works of Tolstoy, Dostoievsky, Turgenev and the like, this is to be taken as a reflection of my own political inclinations.

In sober truth, what happened was this. I subscribed for a number of months to a books-by-post scheme whereby the Masters of English Literature were brought to my door at a phenomenally low cost. When the Masters of Eng. Lit. were exhausted, the computerised firm operating the scheme switched to the Masters of Russian Literature racket, but did not trouble to remove my name from the computer. Indeed, they claim that it is impossible to do so, and that the only way I can stop these books arriving is by hanging myself, when they will automatically be re-routed to my next-of-kin.

These books are not in Russian anyway, they are in finest, good-to-handle skivertex.

3. *London Airport, astonishing number of visits to when not going anywhere.* I often wondered, when catching a glimpse of myself in the television-scanners at Heathrow, whether I ought to come clean with the firm which trades in credit information on individuals about this discrepancy in my movements, as I can see that it must have been puzzling for them. BEA, BOAC, El Al, Pan Am, TWA, Lufthansa, and the People's Airline of the Democratic Republic of Bulgaria have all confirmed that I have not bought an air ticket since God knows when. So what, asked the computer, was I doing mooning about No. 2 Air Terminal for weeks on end? Replying to its own question, it concluded that I was casing the joint.

This is not an accurate assessment of the facts. The trouble with the television-scanner at Heathrow is that it is set at such an angle that it can only reflect a waist-high image. If it had got me in long-shot it would have seen that I was clutching the hand of a small boy called Henry. Henry is a keen aircraft-spotter. I took Henry to London Airport on several occasions as a favour to his daddy who is a friend of mine. The name of his daddy is Beasley. It is not true that I was using Beasley's son as a lever in my attempt to blackmail him.

4. *Explosive weapon, stated intention to manufacture an.* This is laughable. If the firm which trades in credit information on individuals would take the cloth out of its ears and play back the tapes of the telephone conversation to which this accusation refers, it would see that I was talking about a certain winner at Kempton Park and that I said I was going to make a bomb. This conversation was held with Beasley. I did not threaten to bleed Beasley white if he refused to help me manufacture an explosive device. I said, as the computer well knows, that if he did not come in with me he would bloody regret it.

I trust that I have now cleared up these matters to your satisfaction. I was going to ask you to reconsider the mortgage question, but since starting this letter I have had a report from a firm which trades in credit information on building societies. Having skimmed through the relevant documents it tells me that your office is a cover-up for a gang of white-slavers who are the ringleaders of the cocaine-running syndicate with which the Singapore Mafia hope to bring Red China to its knees.

Send me £6,000 in used notes and we'll say no more about it.

Generals by hindsight

The frustrating quarrel between Montgomery and Tedder having been settled, the strategies of the Western Alliance had finally been allowed to go forward. Auchinleck had long ago succeeded Wavell; Alexander had succeeded Auchinleck. The war, not to beat about the bush, had in fact been over for about two and a half years. But there remained the onerous and responsible task of winning the peace.

In the winter of 1948 I was asked by the Air Ministry to go to No. 417 Maintenance Unit, Market Harborough, near Bridgnorth, Salop, to see what contribution I could make towards certain mopping-up operations. My task was to remuster as stores clerk (for I had at last been relieved of the thankless duty of coke orderly) and assist in the shifting of twelve thousand obsolescent hub-caps from the disused balloon hangar near the sports field to the scrap dump behind the corporals' Naafi. For my own part in this operation I naturally accept complete responsibilty, but it would be ungenerous not to put on record that I was assisted, in the early stages at least, by twelve other stores clerks, fourteen aircraftmen second class (general duties) and an itinerant crew of members of the RAF Regiment who were awaiting demob. The name of Leading Aircraftman Roberts comes to mind as one of my colleagues in this enterprise. Roberts went on to take part in the major grass-cutting operation at RAF Station Bicester,

Oxfordshire, while for my sins I remained in limbo and wasted a full six months polishing the fire buckets in the officers' mess annexe—but that is another chapter.

My masters in the hub-cap operation were Corporal Haggerty and Sergeant Grice. In the chain of command I was immediately responsible to Corporal Haggerty, and he was responsible to Sergeant Grice. I would like to place Sergeant Grice's contribution to our air defence, or that sector of it concerning the successful transfer of hub-caps to the back of the corporals' Naafi, in perspective. Certainly 'Bighead' Grice's role was a decisive one. Without his drive, leadership and vision it is conceivable that the hub-caps would never have got shifted at all. His theory that instead of stacking them in ammunition boxes and dragging them through the main gates and up past the education hut we should load them in lorries and take a short cut across the sports field was a courageous one; in the event it saved valuable man hours. But he was a man of mercurial temperament and his judgment was not always sound. I recall—it was one Monday in December when I had returned from a snatch of well-earned leave—Sergeant Grice stopping me as I crossed the barrack square and advising me to button my tunic, put my cap on and stop slouching. Had I taken his counsel to heart I would certainly have put myself at grave odds with my colleagues in No. 4 Barrack Block, with a resultant undermining of my position as billet orderly. Grice, for all his flair, was unable to take the broad view, and it came as no surprise to me that in the peace-time reshuffle his nomination as lift attendant at Selfridge's was vetoed.

Corporal Haggerty was a man of vastly different qualities. I had first known him as a leading aircraftman during the crucial snow-shovelling drive at No. 2 Training Squadron, Skipton-upon-Swale, Yorks, in the previous year. I had been impressed then by his shrewd, tactician's mind and by his willingness to delegate responsibility. I recorded at the time: ' "Ginger" Haggerty has discovered some disused ablutions near the WAAF lines. While the rest of us shovel snow until we are blue with cold, he skives off for a crafty smoke.' He was a man of iron nerve who placed complete faith in the loyalty and sheer know-how of his colleagues. He was physically fit—before being asked to join our team he had been a brilliant chucker-out at the Majestic Ballroom, Stockport—and would not have hesitated to deal summarily with anyone whose allegiance might have been in doubt.

I was delighted to be working with 'Ginger' Haggerty again. From the outset the modus operandi of the hub-cap exercise was bedevilled by conflicting strategies and diverse opinions. Was LAC Roberts's 'private army' of RAF Regiment types entitled to a twenty-five minute break after loading four ammunition boxes on the lorry? Did 'Skiver' Twelvetrees really have a sprained wrist? Was a billet orderly entitled to report for duty as late as 11.30 am? Such thorny questions of protocol dogged the entire RAF effort at that time. It is true that Sergeant Grice cut through the red tape with his now famous dictum: 'You play fair by me and I'll play fair by you, you don't play fair by me and your feet won't touch the ground.' But it was left to the shrewd Haggerty, with his wider experience in the field and his contempt for all things administrative, to come to the real crux of the matter. My journal recalls his words: *'Stuff this for a game of candles. You don't get any medals for working harder.'* This characteristically blunt summary of our situation made a deep impression on me. And on the first day of Operation Hub-cap, Corporal Haggerty having discovered privily that there was to be no roll-call on work-parade (the semi-informal ceremony with which we always began the day's chores), I was delighted to fall in with his suggestion that—again I quote him verbatim— we should 'have it away.'

It is easy now, nineteen years after the event, to say as some 'armchair pundits' have indeed said, that that was where I made my first error of judgment. Hindsight makes generals of us all. I still believe that my assessment of Corporal Haggerty's sagacity and experience was sound. My assessment of his good faith was, unfortunately, not.

While the hub-cap squad toiled Haggerty and I went, my journal records, to Birmingham, where we were able to relax for a few hours at the Odeon cinema. It is still impossible for me to witness a re-screening of 'Ma and Pa Kettle Go To Town' without it conjuring up the smell of chrome and rust, the voice of Sergeant Grice urging his team on to greater efforts, and the vision of LAC Roberts and the 'Crime squad,' as we dubbed his unorthodox army of RAF Regiment personnel, loading ammunition boxes. I have a copy of Robert Browning's *Saul* by me as I write. *'Oh, our manhood's prime vigour! no spirit feels waste, Not a muscle is stopped in its playing, nor sinew unbraced.'* Those lines sum up for me the whole spirit of No. 417 Maintenance Unit at that period.

During the entire first phase of the hub-cap enterprise Corporal Haggerty and I repaired daily to Birmingham, passing our time in cinemas and in the 'pin-table saloons' used mainly by the local population. At about 5 pm on the third day, however, while Haggerty and I were enjoying a cup of tea at a railway station buffet, I noticed something which caused me 'furiously to think.' It is worth quoting from my journal:

'On New Street Station today Haggerty and I saw LAC Roberts, "Skiver" Twelvetrees, A.C.1's Bentley and McDougal, and A.C.2 Norris, all of them the worse for drink. They have all taken a leaf from our book and have been dodging the column. Corporal Haggerty, unwisely in my view, attempted to put them all on a charge. They told him without mincing words to "get knotted." LAC Roberts then sang an obscene song, I am very worried.'

Nor was that all. Back at camp Corporal Haggerty made discreet inquiries among our colleagues. At about seven o'clock that evening he called on me at my bed-space in No. 4 Barrack Block. His demeanour was grave. Out of a total complement of 41 personnel, only seven had reported for duty that morning. The 'powers that be' were alarmed at the apparently slow progress of the transfer of hub-caps from the disused balloon hangar, and an all-out drive would be required if the hangar were to be made ready for the officers' barn dance at the beginning of March— a factor completely new to me, and another example of Maintenance Command's insensitivity to the frustrations of 'working in the dark.' As a first step Sergeant Grice proposed to call the nominal roll at work parade each morning, and to charge any missing personnel with being absent without leave. No quarter would be given; the time for 'soft-pedalling' was long past. Smoking Woodbine after Woodbine, Haggerty informed me flatly that he proposed to fall in with this new arrangement. He urged me to do the same.

Subsequent errors of judgment apart, I have no doubt in my mind that Corporal Haggerty's counsel on that occasion was 100 per cent 'on target.' The following morning he and I were among only five members of the team who reported for duty. The other 36 had their names taken, they were charged with being AWOL and with conduct prejudicial to the good order and discipline of the Royal Air Force, and they were subsequently required to be confined to barracks for seven days. For our part, Haggerty and I were able for the first time to get worthwhile first-hand experience of the loading, transportation and deloading of hub-caps, knowledge that was to be of inestimable value during the surplus gas-cape adventure of 1949.

I have no access to the official files and so I am unable to gauge the anxiety then in the mind of the Air Member in respect of the successful transfer of obsolescent hub-caps. Certainly the barn dance project was a factor. Whether it was a decisive one I am now inclined to doubt. Writing again with hindsight, I am inclined to think that Sergeant Grice—although undoubtedly influenced by the Cabinet's determination to get the hub-caps positioned once and for all behind the Corporals' Naafi—had adopted the operation as his own 'baby' and that it was a matter of personal pride with him to complete the mission before Easter. On the night subsequent to that first roll-call he called his team to an urgent conference on the barrack square. He seemed at first to be in waggish mood and he insisted on us all doubling round the square three times before he would settle down to business. Upon getting down to 'brass tacks,' however, he impressed upon us the seriousness of the situation. He laid great stress upon us all being at work parade the following morning. He reminded us again of his great reputation for fairness and—a typically Griceian *non sequitur*—observed that although we might frighten our mothers we would not frighten him (Grice). It was a chastened body of men that returned to No. 4 Barrack Block at 10 pm.

Corporal Haggerty, however, was not to be disheartened. At 10.30 pm, shortly before lights out, he paid a further visit to my bed-space. Before going to bed I wrote in my journal:

'"Ginger" Haggerty came in this evening and tried to borrow ten shillings. He told me not to take Grice's strictures too seriously. After this morning's *coup de main* over the roll call, undoubtedly every member of the team would muster for work tomorrow. A further roll call would be unnecessary, and I could, if I thought it judicious, skive off to Birmingham for the day without fear of reprisals.'

It is here where the 'armchair strategists' and I are at once. I should either have lent Haggerty the ten shillings or I should have disregarded his hitherto sound advice. The rest is history. That 'Bighead' Grice was duty sergeant the following morning; that in consequence the work parade was taken by Corporal Haggerty; that despite his assurances to me on the previous evening the nominal roll was called; that I was the only absentee; and that I was placed on a charge by Corporal Haggerty, whom I had previously regarded as guide, philosopher and friend, are facts too well known to be repeated. My subsequent disgrace, and the to my mind disproportionate sentence of 14 days' C.B., are still memories too painful to disturb. The Air Ministry, I do not say for political reasons, have never seen fit to re-examine the files on my case. An act of savage injustice has remained on public record. This is my considered opinion nearly twenty years after the event. I have since had plenty of opportunity of thinking over my experience with Maintenance Command and I have seen no reason to change my views. Undoubtedly, I should have lent Haggerty his ten shillings; I had done so before and it was a strategical blunder not to do so again. In this respect, I was wrong. Equally undoubtedly, he acted from motives of self-interest in placing me on a charge, and his action did little to enhance the RAF effort in general or the hub-cap fiasco in particular.

Haggerty has now reached the high position of traffic warden in the St. James's area of London. Needless to say, our paths do not cross.

We don't want to lose you

1. I was instructed by your goodselves to investigate the circumstances surrounding the resignation from the Eyeglass and General Insurance Co. of Mr. Charles Hopcraft Butterfield, with a view to assessing his suitability for employment as an assistant cashier at your Enfield branch.

2. Mr. Butterfield attended Lady Anne Boleyn Grammar School and joined Eyeglass and General in a junior capacity at the age of sixteen on September 4, 1935. He rose to become a senior clerk and resigned at 11.14 a.m. on Wednesday last.

3. I sought an interview with Mr. Butterfield's immediate employer, a Mr. R. Hargreaves, manager of the Approved Claims dept., who sent a message via the commissionaire that it was not Company policy to discuss individual employees.

4. The commissionaire admitted kicking Mr. Butterfield down the office steps on the occasion of his resignation (para 12 refers) but regretted that Company policy precluded him from telling the whole story.

5. Mr. Hargreaves' secretary, a Miss J. Briggs, informed me telephonically that although it was not Company policy to provide Mr. Butterfield with a reference, she would be more than willing, in a personal capacity, to give evidence in the event of the case coming to court. I was unable to pursue this line of inquiry as Miss Briggs was sobbing and laughing.

6. I understand that Mr. Butterfield's own account of his resignation is already known to your goodselves. He was sitting at his desk at 11.08 a.m. on Wednesday last when he suddenly thought he would resign. He sought an interview with Mr. Hargreaves, which was immediately granted, and informed his superior of his decision. Mr. Hargreaves generously waived the four weeks' notice to which the company is legally entitled, and by 11.14 a.m. Mr. Butterfield had cleared out his desk, said good-bye to his colleagues and was on his way out of the office. He recalls that his trouser seat might have just caught against the commissionaire's boot.

7. While having no reason to doubt Mr. Butterfield's word in this matter, I thought it incumbent upon me to make further inquiries. In the first instance I interviewed Mrs. Butterfield, whose statement (attached) I summarise as follows: —

8. Mr. Butterfield had not informed his wife that he intended to resign his position, and the first she knew about it was when he came home at lunchtime on Wednesday last and threw his hat in the fireplace. Asked what was wrong, he replied, 'Sod the lot of them.' Asked to elucidate, he replied, 'They can all go and stuff themselves.' He spoke of having given the Company the best years of his life, adding that one Leonard Hubert Clegg (a senior colleague; see para 12) was an object usually associated with the evacuation of the bowels. Mrs. Butterfield recollects that her husband had previously expressed dissatisfaction with his appointment in 1949, when Mr. Clegg was promoted over his head. She believes that this engendered a sense of grievance which impelled him to seek fresh employment.

9. I next proceeded to the Fox in Boots public house, where Mr. Butterfield is known to have taken refreshment during the hours of 1-3 and 5.30-10.30 on Wednesday last. The landlord, T. Corrigan, states: 'Charles Hopcraft Butterfield is known to me. He arrived at approximately 1 p.m. on Wednesday last and commenced to drink draught lager. I passed the remark that he was an early bird. He

vouchsafed that I was behind the times and that he and the Insurance Company had parted brass rags. Mr. Butterfield further stated that the pot had been coming to the boil for some time now, and that the Company was not big enough for himself and two colleagues whom he mentioned by name, a Mr. Hargreaves and a Mr. Clegg. While he (Mr. Butterfield) had been urging a long-term programme of expansion and diversification, especially in emergent Africa, they (Mr. Hargreaves and Mr. Clegg) were jumped-up office boys who did not understand the nature of modern business. It had finally been amicably agreed that he should be released from his contract and he was now thinking of going free-lance.'

10.   Acquaintances of Mr. Butterfield who were present at the Fox in Boots at the relevant times confirm the landlord's evidence in substance, but differ in some respects as to Mr. Butterfield's future plans. These, summarised, were (a) that luckily he had sufficient funds to enable him to look around for a while; (b) that he was considering an offer from the Prudential as a sort of roving ambassador, going to emergent Africa and other places; (c) that the open-air life was for him and he intended to become a window-cleaner; (d) that he proposed to write a book on the lines of Parkinson's Law, exposing incompetence in the insurance game; and (e) that with the right partner he might consider opening a really high-class restaurant in the vicinity of Rayners Lane tube station.

11.   At the request of your goodselves, I interviewed Miss Colleshaw of the Worldwide Employment Bureau, through whose good offices Mr. Butterfield became aware of the vacancy at your Company's Enfield branch. Miss Colleshaw formed the impression that Mr. Butterfield had severed his connection with Eyeglass and General because of his dissatisfaction with the prospects of promotion. He spoke to Miss Colleshaw of dead men's shoes and remarked that whereas it might suit his colleagues Mr. Hargreaves and Mr. Clegg to be consigned to the scrapheap at aged sixty, it did not suit him. Miss Colleshaw was impressed by Mr.

Butterfield's drive and by his willingness to take the first job offered to him, namely, vegetable chef at the North Thames Gas Board staff canteen, Hendon.

12. In the course of these inquiries I was repeatedly approached by one Leonard Hubert Clegg, described as an under-manager in the employ of the Eyeglass and General Insurance Co., who insisted on making the following voluntary statement: 'I am engaged to Miss J. Briggs, secretary to the manager of the Approved Claims dept., Mr. Hargreaves. On the morning of Wednesday last at approximately 11.03 a.m., Miss Briggs had occasion to enter the stationery cupboard with the purpose of drawing a new blotter. While reaching up to the top shelf she became aware of a hand up her skirt, immediately recognising it by its clammy texture as that of Charles Hopcraft Butterfield. This was the eleventh occasion on which such an assault had taken place. I frogmarched Charles Hopcraft Butterfield into Mr. Hargreaves' office and he was peremptorily dismissed. He was helped on his way by the commissionaire, who happens to be Miss Briggs's uncle. I realise that this statement may constitute a serious slander against Charles Hopcraft Butterfield.

13. I did not form a favourable impression of Mr. Clegg, whose account of Mr. Butterfield's resignation differs substantially from those of the other witnesses interviewed. However, I put Mr. Clegg's allegations to Mr. Butterfield who immediately refuted them, confirming that Mr. Clegg was jealous of him and had always had it in for him. Mr. Butterfield suggested that I should ask of Mr. Clegg what had happened to the sports club tea money last August; this, however, I regarded as outside the scope of my investigation.

14. I am satisfied, after exhaustive inquiries, that Mr. Butterfield resigned from Eyeglass and General for the reasons stated, namely, in the vernacular, that he had had it up to here. Like Miss Colleshaw, I was impressed by Mr. Butterfield's versatility and by his flexible approach to the question of his future career. As an example of this flex-

ible approach, I might mention that upon learning that I was a private investigator, Mr. Butterfield immediately expressed interest in joining the firm in any capacity whatever. I believe it has come to the notice of your goodselves that Mr. Butterfield has invested his life savings in my business. Whatever your goodselves may have heard to the contrary from Mr. Clegg, Mr. Butterfield is only a sleeping partner and his nominal position as co-director should in no way impair his efficiency with any Company that may be fortunate enough to retain his services.

15. I have no hesitation whatever in recommending Mr. Charles Hopcraft Butterfield for employment at your Enfield branch.

Now is the time for all good men ...

Well, Mr. Heath, you've laid your cards on the table so I, Tompkins, will lay my cards on the table. We at the Department of Howsyourfather cannot see our way clear to cutting our expenditure by a single brass farthing. Not by so much as your proverbial sausage, and that is straight up.

I, Tompkins, have your memo to hand in which you say in effect: Do not mess me about, lads, I was not born yesterday, cuts I want and cuts I mean to have.

My only reply to that, Mr. Heath, speaking in the absence of my superiors, is: Get some time in. I, Tompkins, was in the Civil Service when Beveridge was a night-cap, as we say round these parts, and I am telling you that when you have been in this game as long as what I have, you will save your breath for blowing your tea with as regards requests to modify current estimates in a downward direction.

The Department of Howsyourfather has made strenuous efforts to comply with the Prime Minister's earnest desire for economies compatible with the Department's irrevocable future commitments. I am quoting now from a memo what Mr. Netherbridge, who is no doubt familiar to you as our guvnor, has left on his desk. The area of carbon paper, the area of bulldog clips, and the projected scheme to build a £57,000,000,000 computerised sewage farm in the New Forest have all been carefully examined but oh no, the only sodding economy the whole bleeding Department can come up with is to dispense with the services of I, Tompkins.

I, Tompkins, wish to submit a minority report disagreeing with this.

In my grade, which is senior messenger (established) with special responsibility for emptying Mr. Netherbridge's intray, make his tea, wipe his nose etc. etc., I, Tompkins, am getting in the region of twenty nicker a week. Why are we waiting, you may merrily chant Mr. Heath, twenty nicker is twenty nicker in this day and age, get your cards, Tompky lad, every little helps.

Stand on me, Mr. Heath; it is not as simple as that otherwise I would draw my redundancy tomorrow and eff off out of it. It is I, Tompkins's irrevocable future commitments we are talking about now. It is three nippers, mortgage, wife in pod, instalments on electric floor polisher also Christ knows what else. Up yours, you might well ripost, get round the Labour same as what others have to do when the deflation brake has to be applied. Do what the Pakkies do, you might well urge, draw your benefits and put them in your back sky-rocket, no questions asked.

Ho, yes, Mr. Heath, I can see that going down a treat when Harold gets on your tail as regards Tory broken promises. I can just see you in No. 10, waiting for the lads to roll up with their reviews of departmental expenditure. Right, next for shaving, says you, ho, it's you is it Netherbridge, have you implemented them cuts like what I told you? Yes sir, says Netherbridge, we have made a swingeing economy of twenty crisp oncers per week. Twenty nicker! you ejaculate, I have seen better cuts implemented off the Sunday joint, still you done your best Netherbridge, tell Sir Keith Joseph to step in.

In comes Sir Keith with the social securities ledger under his arm. Let us have a skeg then, Keithy, says you, upon which you start effing and blinding all over the shop, also remarking, Streuth! Can't you do nothing right? I am asking you to de-escalate your budget, you berk, not bloody well escalate it, what is that extra item of twenty nicker per week? Ah well, PM, says Sir Keith, that would be Tompkins's benefits.

Right, you may retort to I, Tompkins, it is all down to you Tompky, we in Government have been sweating blue bricks to get the economy on an even footing, how about doing your share, cannot you get by with a few tosheroons less?

I wish I could, Mr. Heath sir, and that is a fact. Strenuous efforts have been made, but regret to advise you that twenty nicker is the bare minimum what I, Tompkins, three nippers and wife in pod can live off of.

The area of fags, booze, subscription to *Our Dogs*, nippers' pocket money and instalments on electric floor polisher have all been examined with negative results, as has also the area of preserves. We are big jam-eaters, always have been, and it is in the direction of Robinson's golliwog that I, Tompkins, have been expecting results. The snag is, Mr. Heath, that wife in pod has taken a big fancy to strawberries. Strawberries she must have, as well as a piece of coal to suck which is why we are unable to revise fuel estimates till November 18 approx. So. Knock strawberry preserves on the head, thus effecting an economy of three-and-a-bit per week, and what happens? Wife in pod is immediately whining for fresh strawberries flown in from bleeding California. If wife were not in pod she would feel the back of I, Tompkins's hand, but as you well know, Mr. Heath, if it is not one exigency it is another.

Area of fags—have tried cutting down to ten per day, but have found this leads to spiralling in Polo mint and Quality Street allocations.

Area of booze—have discovered that reduced intake of Double Diamond is parallel to reduced efficiency in emptying Mr. Netherbridge's in-tray, making tea, wiping nose etc. etc.

Area of instalments on electric floor polisher—have made every effort to rescind HP agreement with Busby's Electrical Stores Ltd., but with sod-all effect. You signed for the swine, you pay for it, says Busby's. What shall I tell Mr. Heath then? queries I, Tompkins. Stuff Mr. Heath replies Busby's, anyway he is in the same boat as regards Trans-Pennine motorway, new Ministry of Transport computer costing six million nicker etc. etc., they are signed for and he will have to cough up and like it.

As to subscription to *Our Dogs*, also nippers' pocket money, wife in pod reads former and nippers spend latter as if it was going out of fashion, so any economies in that direction would only lead to protracted disputes, which is something I, Tompkins, can do without at my age in life.

So there we go, Mr. Heath, and you cannot say that Tompky has not tried to help you out. It is all back to the drawing-board, you should never have done what you done in making all them promises. However do not let the bastards get you down, there is a bright side, you play fair by me and get me re-established in the Department of Howsyourfather and I, Tompkins, will guarantee personal savings of twelve thousand nicker a year, cross my throat.

Tell us another one Tompky, I can hear you saying, ring the other one it's got bells on it. Stand on me, Mr. Heath, I, Tompkins, mean every word, you would not chuckle. Take the area of holidays. Cost of holiday in Costa del Sol for wife in pod and three nippers would be in the region of two hundred smackers, agreed? Right—they are not bleeding well going. Next item, take the area of new semi-detached house what we was thinking of buying next door to my mother-in-law, cost six and a half grand. Say we put off that expenditure till the economy is on an even keel and we are able to expand, get me? That is a total saving of seven grand for a kick-off. Chuck in another five grand for yacht which I, Tompkins, have decided we cannot afford at this stage, that is twelve thousand nicker saved as promised.

All you have got to do on your side, Mr. Heath, is cancel the Concorde and you are laughing. So when it comes to handing out hereditary peerages, do not come the brown loaf by saying I, Tompkins, never did you no favours.